WHO WILL MAKE US WISE?

WHO WILL MAKE US WISE?

HOW THE CHURCHES ARE FAILING HIGHER EDUCATION

ERIC SPRINGSTED

COWLEY PUBLICATIONS
CAMBRIDGE, MASSACHUSETTS

© 1988 by Eric O. Springsted. All rights reserved.
Published in the United States of America
by Cowley Publications.
International Standard Book No.: 0-936384-63-8.
Cover design by Daniel Thaxton.

Library of Congress Cataloging-In-Publication Data
Springsted, Eric O.
    Who will make us wise? / Eric Springsted.
       p. cm.
    Bibliography: p.
    Includes index.
    ISBN 0-936384-63-8 : $8.95
    1. Church and college—United States. 2. Education,
Humanistic—United States. I. Title.
LC383.S73 1988   88-18971
377'.8—dc19

COWLEY PUBLICATIONS
980 MEMORIAL DRIVE
CAMBRIDGE, MA 02138

Acknowledgements

While in seminary some years ago I wrote my former tutor, Robert Neidorf, Dean of St. John's College, Santa Fe, remarking how similar theological education seemed to a liberal arts education. In his reply he asked me to spell out the observation. I never got around to sending him that explanation; having recently learned of his death I particularly regret that failure since in a very important sense the genesis of this book was his question. I owe him a debt of gratitude for having asked it and for being the sort of man who saw it as important to ask. I also owe thanks to Donald Mundinger, President of Illinois College for his support and encouragement. The backbone of this book comes from a number of meditations for faculty seminars and sermons for chapel that I did at Illinois College on the relation of faith and the liberal arts. President Mundinger not only gave me the chance to present these ideas, but encouraged them. I would like to thank my editor, Cynthia Shattuck, for her excellent and enthusiastic help; a book rarely has such a friend. Chapter four originally appeared in a briefer form as "Theology and the Liberal Arts" in *Theology Today*, in July, 1985 and I thank the editors for permission to publish the revised version. Finally, I owe my wife Brenda gratitude for her patient listening and keen observations. Her experience of liberal education, in many ways different and yet the same as my own, caused me to dig deeper and think harder about education and the many different forms it can take. This book is dedicated to our daughters, Simone, Leidy and Elspeth, whose own liberal education lies ahead.

Cowley Publications is a work of the Society of St. John the Evangelist, a religious community for men in the Episcopal Church. The books we publish are a significant part of our ministry along with the work of preaching, hospitality, and spiritual direction. We desire to provide books that will enrich your religious experience and challenge it with fresh approaches.

CONTENTS

Chapter One

Image and Identity

In its October, 1987 issue *Playboy* magazine ran its annual list of the best "party colleges" in America. To thoughtful minds who in the same year had listened to the educational pronouncements of the Secretary of Education, William Bennett, and who had read the critiques of American education of E.D. Hirsch and Allan Bloom, the *Playboy* issue was another reminder of how far American education has strayed from a true course. The magazine's list, however, raised another issue since it included Mercer University, a premier Southern Baptist institution. Not only was there a question of education to be raised in the case of Mercer, there was also the question of Christian education. Mercer is not alone in needing to be asked an important question. That question is, to what degree is the educational image presented by American universities and colleges actually in accord with their real identity? In the case of church-related schools, which claim to be offering something more than secular education, the question is especially pointed.

It has often been claimed that Americans have a particularly strong love affair with education. As with all love affairs, it has its good and bad times. Presently the affair is rocky. Educators wring their hands over the inadequate preparation and literacy of elementary and high school students. Colleges, while bemoaning the miserable preparation of entering students, are scrambling to revise their curricula in order to restore some sense of coherence to the way they educate their students. A shrinking pool of applicants forces them to "market" themselves in order to attract "consumers." The same colleges have also come under heavy criticism for the moral vacuum in which they have allowed their students—and graduates—to exist. Such inadequacies have not gone unnoticed by either private or government agencies, whose criticisms receive constant attention in the press.

American Christianity has not remained on the sidelines in this crisis, particularly on the question of the place of values in education—and what values are taught. At one end of the spectrum, fundamentalists are charging that public education now teaches an alternative religion, secular humanism. Such charges are not groundless: to the degree that public education cannot and does not offer any form of traditional religion, Christian or otherwise, as a living option to students, what values it does have to offer, far from being transcendent, are strictly natural. This, of course, goes further against the grain of the fundamentalists. While the absence of traditional Christian teaching in public schools does not prove by itself that there is such a thing as a religion of secular humanism, there is some historical basis to the charge. John Dewey himself, the major architect of American public education, coined the term secular humanism to describe the common ideology—the "common faith"—he believed was necessary for the functioning of education. For Dewey this common faith was a decided alternative to the traditional forms of religion, which he found to be no longer credible.

It is important to take seriously Dewey's point about education's need for a common faith. It is also important to recognize that he did not invent the notion, since a common faith of some kind has always been at the basis of general education. It was just as true of the ancient Greeks and medieval liberal arts tradition as it is today. The only question is, what will that faith be? Since Dewey did not find Christianity believable, it was necessary for him to find another faith that could make sense of the culture into which people were being educated. In his case, it was a faith that was strictly moral and human without any belief in the supernatural. To the fundamentalist mind, that is not acceptable. While it is not just to lay the entire blame at Dewey's doorstep, nevertheless we have to ask just what common faith does lie behind an educational system. The faith may only be implicit—it is to Dewey's credit that he spelled out his version—but it is undoubtedly there.

In the particular court cases that fundamentalists have brought against the teaching of secular humanism in the public schools, their bill of specifics has often obscured this point to their critics. Generally, their wholesale rejection of Darwinism has made their case against secular values look like one more instance of ignorant and fanatic religious dogmatism. Fundamentalists have also looked ridiculous when they have tried to get a book such as *The Wizard of Oz* banned on the grounds that it allows that some witches are good, or because they have contended that schools teach gun control, which is, they think, forbidden in the Bible.

The point that secular humanism is an alternative religion to Christianity, fundamentalist or otherwise, has not, however, been entirely missed. Richard John Neuhaus, a Lutheran theologian, has argued that "secular humanism is not just a scapegoat or bugaboo of the religious right, but a comprehensive, self-identified view of life that functionally plays the role of a religion." Many professed secular humanists have responded that the omission of any reference to a deity in textbooks does not constitute the teaching of secular humanism as such, and that American public education is neutral because it does not openly advocate secular humanism or any other religion. That surely is the attempt. Yet as Dewey himself noted, any general education is an education in values as well as facts; indeed, we choose to teach the facts we do because of the values we hold and those facts explicitly and implicitly reinforce the values. Thus neutrality on certain values and not others is tantamount to an admission that those values we are neutral about are not really that important to our ongoing life, while the ones that are continually taught are important. Neuhaus has charged: "Censorship by omission is just as pernicious as censorship by commission. It's saying that important questions about life can be answered without reference to religion." Concluding, he then makes the crucial comment, that the issue raises "very solemn and serious questions that are going to be with us a long time, questions about what values, beliefs and purposes we're going to transmit to the next generation."[1]

For the most part the debate about secular humanism has been confined to education in the public elementary and secondary school systems of the United States. But Neuhaus' last comment indicates that the really important question is a matter of much broader scope, and one that is not confined to fundamentalists. Indeed, it is a crucial one for all denominations and educational institutions, particularly for those numerous colleges and universities that traditionally have had, and have sought to maintain, close ties with Christianity. These are schools that exist midway between the fundamentalist Bible colleges and the state universities, which have always sought to teach the best of human knowledge freely and openly while remaining in the light of Christianity.

The example of Mercer shows it is a crucial issue, but not a very clear one. Despite the attempts of some Georgia Baptists to paint the school as a den of utter iniquity, students themselves resisted the characterization and claimed that they were getting an education better than most places offered, including one that did allow for an education in Christianity. For fundamentalists, the issue of religion and education is very sharp; consequently their response has often been simply to separate from the larger culture and to conduct their own type of education, which sometimes includes basing their natural sciences on the Book of Genesis. But that has never been a real alternative for the numerous colleges of mainline

Protestantism, Catholicism and even some evangelical colleges that have tried to be open to contemporary knowledge. These colleges have a twofold calling—to maintain an identity that is essentially Christian while at the same time welcoming the best of the culture in order to transform it in the light of the Gospel. It is hardly an easy task. The lines between the various elements are not always clear, nor is there any ready-made answer to how such colleges might remain true to their calling. In part that is their virtue: by facing it as institutions, they educate students to face it as well. It is not surprising, however, that from time to time the way they face it is not ideal. At present, many of these schools are undergoing a crisis of identity in regard to their relationship to the Christian churches from which they originally sprang, their role in the lives of their students and in the society at large. The problem is less one of trying to exist midway between dogmatism and secularism, since dogmatism is rarely viewed as attractive, but of finding a way to see themselves as grounded in Christianity.

The current tension within the Christian colleges and universities is, in fact, an odd historical twist. Originally both the availability and shape of American higher education was due to the enthusiasm of the Christian churches for learning and to the sense of Christian vocation within the colleges themselves. Virtually all of the colleges founded in the American colonies, with the exception of the University of Pennsylvania, were avowedly Christian. It is ironical now to think of Harvard as a Puritan institution, Princeton as a Presbyterian one, Columbia as an Anglican outpost or Brown as Baptist, yet at one time each of these schools took that relationship very seriously. The strong bonds between the churches and higher education can further be seen in these statistics. By 1861, 162 permanent colleges (i.e. schools that survived the difficulty of establishing themselves) had been established (only twenty-nine of them before 1830). Of these schools, the Presbyterians could claim forty-nine, the

Methodists thirty-four, the Baptists twenty-five, and the Congregationalists twenty-one.These four were simply the denominations with the largest number of colleges.[2]

The numbers, however, only tell a small part of the story. The various different reasons why the churches founded these colleges, when taken together, tell a much greater part. These reasons were essentially threefold. First, when most of these colleges were founded the country had just gone through the Second Great Awakening and the churches were anxious to maintain and increase its influence, especially on the western frontiers. Second, there was a great need for colleges that would train clergy. Third, and just as important, was the churches' desire to civilize the frontier and bring to it the intellectual culture of which the West is heir.

In order to understand the heritage of the Christian liberal arts in this country and its present dilemma, it is important to realize that the desire to bring learning was just as important to the founders of these colleges as their intent to train Christians. When missionaries on the frontier wanted to establish a college or "seminary of learning," they did not simply pick any pious person who could read and write to serve on its faculty; usually they requested young graduates from the best East Coast schools, such as Yale and Princeton. The college presidents in office before 1840 numbered thirty-six Yale graduates and twenty-two Princeton graduates. This emphasis on learning is important because, contrary to what fundamentalists think, it shows that few people who sought to establish piety on the frontier saw knowledge as any threat to Christianity. We can see this by observing how these early colleges operated. Although chapel attendance was required, few schools were sectarian; rather, they tended to be ecumenical, looking to serve the interests of their local communities as much as the interests of their founding denominations. Their prestige heavily contributed to community prestige as well, being the only secondary education available in the geographical area. Furthermore, their form of education was not narrowly biblical; while students were expected to know their Bible thoroughly, that was not all they were expected to know. Instead, they were expected to become, as the ideal of so much of the West from the time of Plato onwards would have it, "whole men." They were to achieve excellence in all their faculties, including intellectual, moral and spiritual, and were to participate fully in the life of the culture and community.

This sort of education can be illustrated by the curriculum generally used in most colleges, with some individual modifications, from the late colonial period up through the middle of the nineteenth century. This curriculum was markedly humane, with a great deal of instruction in Latin and Greek, and later in reading Latin and Greek authors. These authors were read because of the eternal truths they were thought to contain—truths which, it was generally understood, were an essential intellectual frame work for any educated person. Mathematics was also very important; it, too, "trained the mind." This curriculum, therefore, for the most part followed the pattern of liberal arts education begun in the medieval period and like the medieval liberal arts curriculum, languages and mathematics in the latter part of a student's education was replaced by studies in science, philosophy, social science and theology. To a great extent, however, the first three of these subjects were not taught as technical sciences, as we would teach them today, but as "natural philosophy," "moral philosophy" and metaphysics. Generally, one's education was then capped by a course given by the president of the college—usually a minister—which was broad enough to include most major philosophical and religious questions and often titled something like "Natural Evidences of Christianity." Designed to integrate everything that one had been learning to that time, the course invariably featured a distinct blending of Christian faith and the powerful ideas of the Enlightenment.

There are a number of remarkable features about this form of education which we ought to notice, particularly since they

say something about the relationship of Christianity to culture. In the first place, this curriculum was an obvious and
deliberate continuation of a tradition begun with the ancient
Greeks. However, at its best, that continuation was no mere
aping of the ancients, but its fruition. Many cultured people
of the time simply did not see their world as so very different
from the ancient one; where there were obvious differences,
such as new advances in science, rather than overthrow tradition educators tried to incorporate the new ideas into the old.
Second, the form of this curriculum reflected an obvious
belief that human knowledge is a unity and hence that all its
disparate parts can be harmonized into one. Not only was the
curriculum meant to reflect the unity of human knowledge
and the integration of Christian faith with it, the curriculum
itself could create a sense of that unity in the minds of students. So far from being at war with culture, the Christian
liberal arts clearly based themselves on the idea that to bring
students to intellectual culture would be to deposit them on
the very doorstep of Christianity.

Now all of that has changed. There are undoubtedly
numerous reasons why, including the widespread seculariza-
tion of the culture and the rise of state universities—although
originally these operated as Protestant institutions and, in
many cases, were founded by the same ministers who founded
the church-related colleges. Two changes in particular,
however, ought to be noted, since they reflect better than
others the sorts of changes that have created a problem of
identity for Christian higher education. These may not be
direct causes, but they clearly represent a disruption of that
original happy unity. I am speaking of changes in the curriculum and the loosening of ties with the founding churches.

The classical liberal arts curriculum underwent a drastic
change in 1872 when President Eliot of Harvard altered the
relatively fixed curriculum of previous days for one that consisted mainly of electives, that is, courses chosen by the students. Eliot's original idea was a good one, since the old

curriculum focused almost exclusively on the humanities while giving short shrift to the sciences, which were developing at a remarkably independent and fast pace. By introducing a system of electives, Eliot believed that more science could be taught and learned and at a much greater depth.

The change to an elective system went nicely with a new emphasis on research that was captivating the mind of educators. Whereas no one before 1711 had ever suggested that the goal of education was the development of new knowledge through research, instead of acquiring the wisdom of the ancients, by the nineteenth century research had become increasingly important. Its value was reinforced by a heavy borrowing from the German university system which had divided universities into departments, that is, groups of professors dedicated to specific research specialties, each with its own methods. American scholars did not simply borrow this system on hearsay, they personally immersed themselves in it. By the beginning of World War I the number of American scholars who had studied in Germany had risen to over 10,000; there were only 300 on the eve of the Civil War. As these professors returned to the United States, wishing to pursue specialities, nothing could have been more congenial to their minds than to establish departments which were reinforced by an elective system. And thus was also begun the system of faculty members undermining one another in order to compete for students and institutional money and prestige.

The consequences of this move toward specialization on the training of the "whole person" became obvious very quickly. The former curricular unity was immediately lost, and the "whole person" began to graduate little or no knowledge in areas that would normally be considered as essential. Largely as a result of this, in the early twentieth century Harvard introduced the "core curriculum," which required that students take courses in a number of broad areas alongside a specialty or "major" in a specific department.

With some allowance for variations, this is the curriculum still followed today in liberal arts colleges.

Now although the core curriculum does an admirable job of combining a liberal education of some breadth with a specific academic discipline, it still lacks the unity prized by the older liberal arts curriculum. Nothing has altered the system of departmental specialities. One place where the effect of this is most noticeable is in the teaching of religion. While most Christian liberal arts colleges maintain a department of religion (or philosophy and religion), and some even require one or more religion courses as part of the "general requirements" the old capstone course taught by the president has disappeared. Now "religion" is one more department among others. Far from serving an integrative function, religious studies is simply one more research specialty like any other. Rarely do we see religion taught as a course that can unify our intellectual and moral education and experience. As a result, the curriculum no longer represents as it did to the founders of the pre-Civil War colleges, the unity of knowledge under a supreme Thinker and moral agent.

Nor is it any longer a means of using intellectual culture to bring students to an awareness of God. "The Bible as Literature," "The Novelist as Religious Thinker" and "Christian Existentialism" are often good and interesting courses; rarely, however, are they courses where the findings and questions raised by other departments are given a treatment testing their contribution to ultimacy. It is then difficult to say what exactly Christian higher education is, since there no longer seems to be any common ground between the education of the intellect and the experience of God. Without this common ground, then, it is even more difficult to say exactly what the identity of a Christian college is.

If the fragmentation of knowledge among departments and elective requirements has weakened the relation between Christianity and intellectual culture in the colleges, it is still not the only culprit. Another sign of the weakened relationship is the fact that many colleges which were originally tied to Christian churches have dropped or loosened considerably their affiliation. There are numerous reasons for this, including the wish to distance the college from unwarranted ecclesiastical interference. Often schools that have gained some prestige in the academic community are wary of being perceived as committed to any sort of dogmatism, which they think will damage their reputations for courageous independent thinking. The apparent shibboleth of our times is the belief that one cannot be Christian and remain at the intellectual forefront of American education. Although most mainline Protestant churches attempt to exercise little or no influence on the colleges to which they are tied, it nevertheless appears to many colleges that advocating explicit Christian faith is a *prima facie* case for the institution promoting a rigid worldview instead of freely applying a critical knife to prejudice. As often as not, the real practical reason is that a lot of intelligent people on these campuses do not want their prejudices challenged.

These weak relations were particularly well illustrated in the case of Macalester College, one of the more prestigious Presbyterian schools. Since its founding Macalester had enjoyed particularly felicitous relations with the local Presbyterian churches, especially the largest one, House of Hope. As a sign of the relationship, the House of Hope at the beginning of the century gave the college a bell from the church when the congregation moved to a larger building. In the 1960's, however, as it gained a national reputation, Macalester began to distance itself from the church and the denomination as a whole; by the 1970's the relations were all but severed, with the school deciding not to replace the chaplain and failing to maintain the House of Hope minister on the board of trustees. Then on a snowy Christmas eve in 1978 the bell mysteriously appeared in the House of Hope chancel, where it greeted the congregation as it came for the midnight service. Having directed his assistant to give it a mighty ring, the minister announced that should the college wish to reestablish its ties with the church, the retrieval of the bell would be a perfect opportunity to do so. He even offered to lead a march of students down the two mile avenue to retrieve it. The college, however, refused to see the humor in the situation and began to mutter threats about legal action. The bell was subsequently returned with little additional warmth arising from the incident.

The transformation of the original liberal arts curriculum has given a subtle message not only to students but to the world outside that intellectual culture does not culminate in theological vision. Loosening of the ties between the colleges and the churches signals a further belief that advancement in learning cannot take place under the auspices of Christianity. Both indicate a further pulling apart of Christianity and intellectual culture. What does this portend for the Christian colleges and their role within the culture and in the church?

On one level, it may mean nothing more than a change in the outer form of the mission of these colleges. Many presidents of Christian liberal arts colleges, for example, would suggest that the colleges still continue to play a distinctive role in religious formation, but one that has adapted itself to the contemporary situation. They can point out numerous ways in which the church-related colleges remain distinctive. These colleges still are midway between the larger (and totally secular) state universities and the small Bible colleges. They still aim at educating the whole person and can produce numerous bits of evidence to back their claim. Such colleges still, for the most part, require a broad exposure in both the humanities and in science, resisting the temptation to become vocational in scope and mission. Some require a course or two in religion, and a surprising number still continue to hold chapel services, although these are rarely required. Above all, in stressing the education of the whole person, the Christian liberal arts schools emphasize "values" both in the form and content of their curriculum and in the social life of the campuses. Presidents will also stress the relatively small size of their schools, which allows for some sort of community to be formed. There is also good evidence that these claims are valid, and the schools actually do most of what they say they are doing.

Yet confusion and anxiety about the role and function of these schools still exists. There is reason to suspect that the image presented to the board of trustees, to the alumni and to the students does not always fit the underlying identity; the role they are playing is not a modern equivalent of the traditional Christian liberal arts. I do not mean to accuse such schools of deliberate misrepresentation. I do mean to suggest that the college's role is often determined by its competition, that is, the secular universities, and that the values by which a college educates are often determined by a culture which is now, by and large, post-Christian. Thus the source of values upon which a college draws may be ambiguous. The problem is one of clarity. As a graduate of one black Presbyterian college put it: "It is a matter of knowing who you are and whose you are."

Let me explain, however, more precisely what I mean by reference to a book that is currently receiving a great deal of attention, Allan Bloom's *The Closing of the American Mind*. Although Bloom nowhere mentions the Christian colleges, his position is particularly instructive for them.

In classical fashion Bloom sees the goal of education as learning to reason and becoming open to what reason can discover. Education, he argues, is the presentation of the best alternatives of life and thought open to a reasonable mind. But it does not stop there. Education should also develop students' ability to reason so that they may come to see these alternatives for themselves and then act on what is truly valuable. In short, education—and the schools where it takes place—ought to furnish an alternative to what is handed out (and accepted) so unreflectively in society at large. Without these alternatives we have few choices that are not dictated either by our passions and whims or by external pressure.

But, Bloom argues, this is exactly what is not happening in education. What has disappeared is not the advancement of scientific knowledge, because there is still plenty of that to go around, but any sort of capacity for reason that genuinely opens us to see alternatives to our pet prejudices. Society has both encompassed and encumbered education; schools are now merely replaying internally the very same unthought out questions, attitudes and values that belong to society at large.

Bloom's particular *bete noir* is the relativism of values that he sees pervading campuses. This relativism is not a matter of students having no values, for they obviously do have values and are often very impassioned about them. Rather it lies in the fact that students no longer see any reason for choosing or for holding the values they, or anybody else for that matter, do hold. They simply hold them. There is probably not a college professor in the country who has not seen some truth in this charge as she reads papers in which the major excuse given for holding a position or opinion is individual perspective on the matter, personal preference, passing whim, or "how I was brought up."

To a certain degree it is always going to be the case that students will arrive at college with individual wants and prejudices, and will rarely be able to spell out the reasons by which they adopt and hold a position. The problem occurs when colleges simply acquiesce in this. In the name of "openness," Bloom thinks, colleges have refused to challenge this relativism; to the degree that they encourage numerous options without challenging any of them, schools have even contributed to it. Ironically, although this neutrality is carried out in the name of openness, actually it is closed-minded. No one ever has to change his opinion about anything. Nor would he be considered "moral" should he invite another person to change; that is "pressure." Consequently students not only resist, as they naturally do, developing the habits of sound, reasonable judgment, they are encouraged in this by the acquiescence of the colleges.

A further result of this relativism within colleges and universities is their inevitable failure to provide any sort of standard of, or basis for, judgment. A standard of judgment allows us to stand somewhat outside the cultural melee and bring critical faculties to bear on the unconscious direction taken by popular culture. Whereas previous generations brought up on the classics could refer to Plato or Cicero as standards of good judgment, today such classics, if read at all, are considered simply one more opinion. Bloom notes the importance of books such as these when he talks about the reversal that has taken place in his own thinking.

During the 1960's, Bloom relates, he felt a certain admiration for the American educational system. Although unlike the products of European systems who were thoroughly trained in Western culture before they reached the university, American students nevertheless dived into their studies with an enthusiasm rarely paralleled by their European counterparts. In the end, they seemed to learn just as much and perhaps did so with more originality. At that time Bloom thought that the adolescent mind indeed loved learning for its own sake and would seize whatever opportunities for learning it could find. However, he notes, that enthusiasm seems lacking in the 1980's. One reason may be that the earlier generation was not the *tabula rasa* it may have seemed, for generally students in the sixties did bring two sources of value with them to college: knowledge and appreciation both of the United States Constitution and the Bible. That, however, is rarely true anymore. The effects are being felt in contemporary education where few students have a source of value, apart from their personal preference, on which to base their judgments.

In many ways Bloom's book, particularly in the examples he chooses, can be seen as a gibe against ridiculous courses

in university catalogues and against social movements on college campuses. Often his criticism of these movements
amounts simply to caricature and serves a politically conservative point. His comments on feminism fail to note that
feminism may be trying in some quarters to restore parts of a
tradition we have lost; his broadside against rock music
makes him sound like a common scold. But there is a deeper
issue to Bloom's arguments: rarely do we see nowadays any
efforts toward the formation of the inner person on the part
of colleges and universities. Education of the "whole person"
turns out to be a superficial exposure of students to a broad
number of courses; there is no significant change of the moral
makeup of these students, however, no attempt to improve
character, from the time they enter to the time they graduate.
What has replaced teaching of the whole person is a modern
sort of sophistry.

The term "sophistry" is an apt one, for both of Plato's
criticisms of the sophists apply. On the one hand, he rebuked
them for having no real basis in knowledge for what they
taught. Rather, he suggests, the art of the sophist is like that
of preparing a good meal; it is a "knack" that comes from experience and simply amounts to having developed a feel for
cooking. But if the sophists' teaching has no real knowledge
behind it, then all that their students can learn is a knack. On
the other hand Plato also accused the sophists—in their
relationship to the culture at large—of being like the trainers
of some great beast. These trainers, with a particularly keen
eye for their own advantage, quickly learn (it is again a
knack) what pleases the beast and what displeases it. Upon
having learned this, they simply call "good" whatever pleases
the beast, and "evil" whatever displeases it.

What is the modern parallel? The so-called "values" which
are so highly touted on college campuses are simply the
prejudices of the society at large. Popular ideas such as
"democracy" and "equality" are rarely questioned; in fact,
questioning of them is not welcomed. Perhaps the best ex-

ample of this lack of questioning occurred in the case of a geneticist in the 1970s who claimed to have evidence for the genetic inferiority of Blacks. Because his findings were controversial, he was frequently invited to speak on college campuses. However, he was rarely heard because student protests forced cancellation of his talk or because he could not be heard over the heckling. Whether he was right or wrong is not particularly an issue, since few ever got to the issue. The sacred name of equality apparently could only be spoken in reverential tones, tones in which open discussion rarely takes place. Ironically, the student refusal was particularly foolish since the sort of equality they wanted to protect was political equality and not intellectual ability. In fact, if he were right a very important issue about the nature of political equality would have to be recognized. The refusal to listen was also foolish because if the man were wrong, few would ever know why or would have learned how to argue effectively against what may have been a dangerous idea. The result? Far from being discredited, the idea may simply be lying in wait for a more reactionary time when it will be taken up with as little reason as it was once rejected.

Bloom, although he does not direct his criticisms specifically to Christian liberal arts schools, nevertheless offers two explicit challenges which these schools must take up. First, they must ask whether or not they are simply following the pattern he describes, despite their claims to the contrary. If they are, the "values" education they are promoting may indeed be quite shallow—it may do no more than encourage the acting out of unreasoned commitments. The question Christian liberal arts colleges need to face, as do all schools, is what values are actually dominant in their form of education? Are they really a modern equivalent of the values they began with, or has there been a shift to acquiescence in unreflective cultural trends?

The second challenge is religious. In an important section of his argument, Bloom suggests that the values of any cul-

ture are essentially religious, meaning that every state has its
own pantheon of gods. Occasionally there are some real gods
in that pantheon; often, however, it is jammed with idols that
leave little room for real gods. What education ought to be is
a means of learning to discern gods from idols. It ought to
present an alternative to those idols. Socrates was condemned
for teaching about gods that were not Athenian, and Bloom
thinks that in this lay his educational genius. Similarly
Nietzche criticized contemporary idols of nineteenth century
culture. Today the idols continue to exist, although rarely do
we have formal ceremonies to honor them. Equality as an ultimate goal, inexorable technological progress, and nationalism are such idols. Not only must we ask, therefore, whether
the Christian schools are providing some alternative to unreflective popular values, we must also ask whether they are
providing the transcendent and deep Christian values that
have always been critical of finite cultural idols? The degree
to which these schools accept the idols of the culture and do
not challenge them is the degree to which their real identity
is that of cultural paganism.

   In order to see the importance of these questions, the importance of presenting an alternative, we have only to look at
the present generation of students. Their attitudes towards education are extremely pragmatic. In varying degrees, students' interest in higher education over the last fifteen years
or so has become increasingly vocational. When given the
chance they have chosen to flock to business administration
courses, although not out of a deep and abiding interest in
business as such. Rather than looking towards their schools
to change them, and to shape them into a certain kind of person, they have often resisted moral change and simply sought
to develop marketable skills. Volunteer activities on many
campuses are at a particularly low ebb. All this is reflected in
the frustration virtually every college chaplain feels in trying
to garner any interest in either religious or volunteer activities. Even in schools with a strong activist bent—protests

against the investment of the college endowment in businesses that are heavily involved in South Africa—this activity rarely shows a corresponding interest in any thing remotely religious. One chaplain in particular, after getting himself arrested with students for occupying the college president's office in just such a protest, still found himself almost entirely alone on the Sunday morning in chapel when he was prepared to speak of his motive for doing so.

One cannot blame schools for the attitudes of a generation of students. Yet educators have not always made strenuous efforts to change those attitudes. In good part this is because challenging those attitudes runs the risk of offending students. Increasingly liberal arts colleges are "market-driven," as they say in American business. Schools which were filled with "babyboomers" twenty years ago must compete for a diminishing pool of applicants now. The example of any liberal arts college which has to close, and many have in the 1980s, has an extremely sobering effect on trustees and presidents. Therefore as students become more oriented to vocational education, many schools have introduced more vocationally specific courses of study, often without any real discussion of how these contribute to the education of the whole person or how they fit into a liberal arts curriculum. The more they do so, the more they come to resemble small state universities. As more students enter state universities, these changes seem necessary for reasons of survival. Nevertheless a school with a majority of students pursuing personnel management cannot help but deflect liberal arts into an education that merely gives a cultured patina to middle management.

This, of course, is not the intention but many schools are in no position to do anything else. Even the faculty, who seemingly worry the most about the quality of education, have an entrenched position to protect. The curricular structure of most colleges revolves around specialized departments, which work against any overall coordination of a student's education, even if she is required to have broad exposure to the various disciplines. Moreover, the form of teaching often simply reflects the bias of an individual discipline, rarely seeking to integrate a student's whole intellectual and moral life. That integration is often left to the chance that the student herself will see how it all coheres. At graduation students are rarely the heirs of their intellectual heritage. Few students when they graduate will even have a passing acquaintance with many of the greatest books of Western culture. The ones they do know of will be some literature, perhaps the Bible, and a few important American documents such as the Constitution. Beyond that, they may have read some snippets from anthologies in other fields. Yet it is extremely unlikely that they will have actually read Herodotus or Thucydides in history courses, Freud or Jung in psychology (although, of course, they will know all about Freud!) or Darwin in biology. What they are missing is the opportunity to see what Thucydides, Freud and Darwin all might have in common, that is, the deepest questions of the Western mind. If a student is not consciously aware of those questions, I would suggest, then the "whole person" has not been reached except in the most superficial way.

The status of religion on campus also raises the question of image and identity for denominational schools. It would not be fair to say that these schools have no interest in their Christian heritage whatsoever; the very fact that they identify themselves as being in some sense Christian indicates that they do. Such schools often have a chaplain and make sure that opportunity exists for worship and religious fellowship. They advertise the fact that religion is an important contributor to the formation of the "whole person." Far too often, in an attempt to be "open" and to ensure the social and cultural happiness of students, they have unwittingly encouraged every merely social option to the detriment of religious life. Incoming freshmen will find fraternities, sororities, clubs and social events; they will be encouraged to become involved in any number of these. The religious activities are merely mentioned for those who may have an interest in them. The message is clear—religious activities are not the most important on campus. The message is also gladly welcomed by students who would rather join the party at some Greek house. Thus many chaplains feel that even should Jesus himself speak at Wednesday chapel, few students would attend unless they were to receive some academic credit for doing so.

Just as schools cannot blame their woes solely on student attitudes, so too the schools cannot bear all the blame themselves for the change that has taken place. The churches to which they are tied must also bear part of it. If the schools twenty years ago did begin to withdraw from the churches, the situation has now changed. Often any live connection that now exists be tween a denomination and a school is the result of the school's efforts. Many Protestant mainline churches have to a great extent neglected their schools. Within the Presbyterian Church, which 120 years ago founded more colleges than any other denomination, few of its seventy colleges still identified as Presbyterian receive as much as one per cent of their budget from denominational support. Yet the problem is not really even a financial one; rather, the denominations tend to ignore the schools and refuse to recognize their problems.

One president of a midwestern university bitterly complains that the regional denominational organization refused to meet at his school until it agreed to participate in a program requiring it to purchase from minority businesses; his hands were tied, since there were virtually no minority businesses in the area. Within the committee on higher education of the same denomination, one member was repeatedly heard to express surprise that the six denominational schools within the area were not Bible colleges! Not only was he unaware of the denomination's colleges, although he was making decisions about them, he also did not seem to be able to keep any information about them in his head. Needless to say he, as many ministers do, was sending his children to state universities for their education. I frequently hear the complaints of faculty members at denominational schools that they are never invited to present programs at local churches, and that their main contact with the local churches is, if they are ordained, simply to fill the pulpit when the minister is on vacation. These examples are simply indicative of the fact that many denominations have been content to let their colleges go their own way.

These are strong reasons to suspect that much of present Christian liberal arts education is simply not the modern equivalent of the older tradition of Christian humanism. Certainly there have been serious attempts to make it such; some schools such as St. Olaf, a Lutheran school, and Calvin, a Christian Reformed school, are noteworthy for their efforts and quality of education. In fact, many of the Christian liberal arts schools remain the wisest choice for entering freshman since whatever problems they may have are no less prevalent at state and private universities. Nevertheless, what seems to be missing is a certain vision of the whole person and how to educate her. For many years that vision was assumed to be the common property of the church and school administrators, faculty and students. Now few are really sure what the tradition really is, although everybody has an opinion. In light of this lack of common understanding churches, administrators, faculty and students also have developed separate agendas for education; nobody is quite sure what role to play. It is small wonder that as each group seeks its own interests, the result is growing doubt about the relevance of the liberal arts to life in the contemporary world.

There are, I suggest, at least three crucial elements to recovering a common vision of the Christian liberal arts so that it may make a significant contribution to education. The first is a sense of who the "whole person" is, especially in light of the Gospel. Whatever else the Christian liberal arts does, it ought to aim at producing this sort of person. Second, it is important to see how that person can be both Christian and intellectually aware, particularly in respect to the academic community in which he or she is educated. Finally, it is crucial to discover what roles the many individuals must play in this education—professors, administrators, chaplains and clergy as well as students. The following chapters are an attempt to bring all these elements together.

Chapter Two

Whose Body?

"Just as the human body, though it is made of many parts, is a single unit because all these parts, though many, make one body, so it is with Christ...You together are Christ's body; but each of you is a different part of it." (I Corinthians 12.12, 27 NJB)

In writing to the dissension-torn Corinthian church in 57 A.D. St. Paul created a striking metaphor for the church that we have used ever since. The church, Paul contends, is like a body. Each believer, with his or her individual gifts, has an essential part to play in the functioning of the whole, as a hand or a foot does in the human body. Despite the fact that the passage is well known, however, it is often not very well understood. Too often we read it from the perspective of our highly developed sense of individualism. We read it as if individuals and their talents exist first, and only then, by "social grouping," compose an abstract entity called the church. But this is not what St. Paul means. Instead, he means to declare the priority of the body over the parts. Believers are first participants in the whole and then have special functions *derived* from that participation. Just as a hand or foot that is cut off from the body is no longer a hand or foot but a mass of flesh, so too special talents cease being real talents unless connected to something larger, from which they draw life. Put another way, there are no individual gifts until one is part of the whole. Thus the importance of each gift and the source of energy necessary to use that gift comes from the whole.

When St. Paul develops this analogy he is, of course, talking about a unique institution, the church. And not only is it unique, it is also divine. But these things not withstanding, there is, I think, an analogy between the church as the body of Christ and societies and schools. This analogy is that in both instances we are first parts of a whole and only later individuals. We are not isolated individuals, but ones who stand upon the whole.

Paul's organic metaphor is an extremely rich one that can have significance for education on a number of levels. It invites us to consider the role of education within the body of the culture at large and it invites us to think about the role of the various people and elements in education. It also compels us to think about how the educated person—the "whole person"—becomes whole and how he or she may be related to a larger body.

Even the most casual survey of the catalogues of liberal arts colleges will reveal that virtually all of these institutions seek to educate the "whole person," or its semantic equivalent. But what exactly is this whole person, anyhow, and how do you educate a student to be one? Apparently it means what the ancient Greeks took it to mean, according to most college catalogues—it means developing the student spiritually, intellectually, culturally, and physically. The curriculum is meant to reflect this intent when it requires broad exposure to the various disciplines of the human mind, allows opportunity for spiritual and physical exercise, and provides numerous opportunities to drink at the fount of culture.

The definition sounds good. There is, however, a problem with this sort of attempt to define the whole person; like Humpty Dumpty, it breaks him into pieces—spirit, brain, body—and somehow does not say how he is to be put back together again. Socrates once complained that when he asked the Athenian general Meno what virtue is, Meno replied by giving him a whole list of virtues instead the one thing that constituted them all. Socrates didn't think Meno's answer was a good one at all; it was like asking for a plate and being given a lot of pieces of a broken one. So it is with being given all the parts of a whole person. What we need to discover is what makes the person whole and unified. Only after that can we begin to divide up and assign the task of educating her. Unless we know how these parts are to be related internally, as well as her place within the larger world, that division is futile.

The Greeks were wiser. What the Greeks meant by the whole person can be seen in their term *paideia*—the root of our word pedagogy. Originally, *paideia* meant simply "child-rearing." However, in time, it also came to mean what we understand by "culture." The connection is not accidental, for in bringing up a child we enable him to take part in cultural life as an adult. For the Greeks, this especially meant enabling a freeman to make political, social and cultural decisions as a citizen. To be an educated person—a person of culture—was by no means to be a dilettante, or a specialist, but to be a person who could be counted upon to make the right kinds of decisions essential for the ongoing life of the community —"the body." He not only possessed certain kinds of knowledge, but also could act upon that knowledge. Most of all, the whole person knew himself to belong to his community, where nothing of value in that community was foreign.

The Greeks in their maturity spent a great deal of time grappling with the issue of how to make someone a person of culture. Plato, for example, devised a curriculum in which students—both male and female, an idea unique to him—by learning athletics for the discipline of the body in order to fight well in battle. Then they learned music so that they would not be brutal and coarse. Next students began a rigorous study of mathematics in order to understand the essential makeup of the physical world, and finally concluded their studies with philosophy in order to discover ultimate principles. Isocrates, who founded a school that competed with Plato, did not follow this philosophical education; instead he stressed training in verbal and rhetorical abilities so that the free citizenry might be able to argue well in political assemblies. Despite the differences between Plato and Isocrates, which often were profound and went to the heart of the question of what Athenian culture should become in the future, both schools shared a common belief that the whole person was a citizen for the community.

Our contemporary versions of the liberal arts are in many ways the continuation of an ideal begun in the Greeks; in fact, the liberal arts tradition is one of the clearest examples of a continuing cultural tradition in the West. Even the idea of educating the whole person to become an effective citizen is still highlighted in official catalogues. Yet despite the rhetoric, there is often a crucial difference between what we say and what the Greeks did. The Greek city state, in good part due to its homogeneity, had reached a much greater consensus on the common good; we, because of our emphasis on cultural pluralism, have a much more difficult time defining what it means to be a citizen. We may even see the attempt to define and enforce a particular cultural form as immoral. The attempt is labelled "cultural imperialism."

Rarely do we even attempt to fit a student anymore to any cultural ideal; instead we have tended to orient her education more towards the development of publicly useful skills, since at least we can agree on those. But the "skilled" person is hardly the same as the whole person, as we can readily see. The skilled person is well trained, and sometimes we might say, even overeducated. She is a person of many facts and formulae, but may be virtually uneducated beyond her area of expertise. One news commentator noted after the drastic stock market drop in October, 1987 when hundreds of budding investment bankers became unemployed, that none of them had any skills that would translate into another line of work. Rarely does the merely skilled person know much about matters outside his field, even matters of crucial importance. This person is a far cry from the Greek citizen who was called upon to be a warrior, a juryman, a singer and an athlete, as well as one who knew his Homer thoroughly and often had to manage an estate. The skilled person is good at providing facts and "agendas" for decisions, and can ultimately be replaced by any other person of similar skills, like a computer chip; the whole person provides judgment and, even if she is not a leader, is still indispensible within a society.

We all recognize the difference between wholeness and mere skill, but in what does it mainly consist? It is clear that we are not simply talking about a matter of factual knowledge; factual knowledge, even when it is broad, will not produce a person of judgment, although a person of judgment cannot do without knowing certain facts. What creates a whole person, I suggest, is a sense of overarching purpose. It lets her know what to do with whatever skills and knowledge she might possess. This moral sense is not something that can be taught, as we would the periodic table or the chronology of British kings, nor is it even a matter of individual knowledge or talent. It cannot be developed by a person alone; it can only come from participating in something larger than herself—her community and her culture. Therefore this sense of moral purpose can only be developed by becoming part of a whole, a community, a "body."

Because we have difficulty recognizing the importance of belonging to a body, we too often assume, perhaps tacitly, that the liberation of students from ignorance consists in the discovery and cultivation of those special talents they bring with them when they come to college. So we hope that under our tutelage students will recognize their own individual talents and then go on to use them for achieving personal success in the world "outside." We hope that these talents, when cultivated, will contribute to the general well-being of everyone within the society. Unfortunately, this philosophy of education is hardly sound educational theory; it is the unwitting adaptation of liberal economic theory to education, for it assumes that special interests—skills and talents—can somehow be played off against each other to the advantage of the whole. We are using a "free market" model, which assumes that by increasing the quantity of individual talents in a society we will increase both the general well-being and the well-being of all individual members as well. Yet there is no necessary relationship between the two. Although the theory has been discredited economically, we have not become any wiser in education.

The fact is that teachers and students are first of all simply human beings, with a long and rich intellectual and moral heritage behind them. We are not individuals with special talents who can insist that the social contract be renegotiated at our births. Instead, we are born knowing nothing. Gradually we learn behavior, and most important of all, we learn language in the broadest as well as the narrowest sense. As the French philosopher Simone Weil put it, because of that language we possess a culture and through that culture we grasp the world. Much as we would like to think otherwise, there is no other way we can grasp the world.

Weil's point that we have culture through language and that we use the language of culture to grasp the world can be illustrated at the simplest level by E. D. Hirsch's argument in *Cultural Literacy*, a book that has recently received a great deal of attention in educational circles. Hirsch argues that the ability to understand language is more than simply "decoding" verbal sounds or written symbols; it also involves possession of a "cultural vocabulary" or "background knowledge." With this vocabulary we are able to sort and categorize what we hear and read into meaningful statements; without it, we fail to comprehend what is being said. The more background knowledge we have, the better we are able to organize and hold onto our knowledge. For example, a group of community college students found reading a passage on Lee's surrender to Grant at Appomattox Courthouse surprisingly difficult to understand, not because the words used in the passage were unfamiliar, but because they did not know who Grant and Lee were. They could define the words well enough; their cultural illiteracy kept the students from putting them into any meaningful context—the passage made almost no sense to them. Our ability to understand what goes on around us is depends on our ability to participate in a culture, in this case represented by a cultural vocabulary.

Possession of a cultural vocabulary is important, but getting hold of the world is more than a matter of content. There is also the need to speak that vocabulary intelligently and with good judgment. We also need a form of language that gives meaning to our utterances and actions. Until we have it, we are barbarians as the Greeks understood the term. "Barbarians" was the name for who couldn't speak Greek—all who did not have *paideia*—because their language constantly sounded like "bar-bar-bar" to cultured Greek ears. It is the function of the liberal arts to teach us how to speak, which is to say, how to participate in the body of the culture and the life of the mind.

Participating wholly in one's culture is crucial and that is why a good liberal arts education cannot really be defined as either "special" or "general." It is first of all a means by which students come to derive their intellectual lives and their understanding of the world from the body of the surrounding culture. This does not mean we should never become specialists or generalists, but we do need to recognize that human beings can only really exercise special talents *after* education, not before. Liberal arts education goes beyond simple utilitarian and pragmatic considerations. It goes to the heart of what it means to be a rational being, and that means that one must first be an intelligent participant in the culture. And not only must students be participants in it, they must learn to draw life from it, just as Paul exhorts believers first to draw life from the body of Christ.

Paul's insistence upon the need for participation in the body, the whole, receives support from another organic metaphor, this time from Simone Weil's notion of rootedness. In her last work, *The Need for Roots*, Weil argued that human beings have certain spiritual needs analogous to bodily needs such as the need for food and shelter. If these needs are not met the spirit withers, just as the body weakens when it is not fed. Chief among these needs, Weil contended, is the need for roots. This is a need to be rooted in a culture, which preserves the important treasures of the past and expectations for the future. Our sense of justice, for example, is something that has been transmitted to us through a tradition that includes the Bible and the Greeks. We appeal to that tradition to justify our actions; without it, our actions lose universal appeal. It is through our cultural roots that we draw most of our moral, intellectual and spiritual ideas and life.

The world into which we are born is one that already possesses a certain amount of order; by learning that order, we make our way in the world with varying degrees of success. At first we have before us only a formally ordered world. Where that world begins to develop deep spiritual significance is when we begin to see that it is through that order that links are created, links by which our lives are forged into a whole, both individually and collectively. A society whose people are well-rooted is one where strictly personal demands are less strident; its citizens can see that their own welfare is linked to the welfare of others. So they have less reason to demand more for themselves. If the culture itself is rooted within the wider world, it can establish links to other peoples and cultures. By embodying both the past and expectations for the future, the culture links the past and future of a people and gives them a place in the world. It lends them spiritual sustenance by giving coherence and purpose to life.

The importance of being rooted is particularly evident when we are confronted with its opposite, uprootedness.

When we are uprooted, Weil writes, we lose the ability to appreciate tested and enduring values. So in time our chief values become those of the lowest common denominator of our society, such as money and power. Recently I came across an example of this sort of uprootedness in an article from *Newsweek*, which described the recent attempt of many MBA programs to institute business ethics courses. It seems their incoming students lack any sort of ability to reason morally. The article included this sample question from a business ethics exam: A drug company has just put a new product on the market. One researcher objects to marketing the product because it received inadequate testing and has probable dangerous side effects. The project director refuses to listen. When the researcher further complains, the director gives the researcher poor job evaluations and seeks to undermine her credibility. Moreover, the researcher is a economically vulnerable—she is a single parent of three children. You are the vice president for personnel and the situation is brought to your attention. What do you do?

Now, the obvious answer is that you fire the project director. Few of the students, however, gave this as an answer; most worried about the effects that disclosure of the product's dangers would have on the price of the company's stock. What is interesting about this response is not so much the fact that they did not "get" the answer or that they were not thinking—actually they thought very hard about it—but that for them ethics meant stock prices and not the just treatment of human beings. For these students, human values had come to be replaced by inhuman ones. It is quite clear that the values of the society that have come down to us from Socrates, Jesus and the like were no part of their mental baggage. These students did not seem to recognize that their participation in the society amounted to anything more than a "bottom line" issue.

The ancient world had something called the *sensus communis*, similar to Weil's and St. Paul's stress on our primary need to derive values from a community by participating in it.[3] *Sensus communis* stands behind our "common sense" but the older term is far richer. It involves not only good practical judgment, but also an appeal to the consensus of the community for moral and aesthetic values. A communal sense, a sense of the common good, is absolutely crucial for building and improving a society and therefore it furnishes a good deal more than a way of coping within a society.

By its very nature the *sensus communis* is nearly impossible to define, since it depends upon the history of the community and the interplay of its various elements. It can, however, be seen in an example that Aristotle provides. In his discussion of justice in the *Nichomachean Ethics* Aristotle provides various mathematical formulae for obtaining justice. If, for example, there are N amount of goods to be distributed, a judge ought to distribute them in proportion to the worth of the plaintiffs. Thus a man who works twice as hard as another on a project ought to get twice as much as the other. However, Aristotle recognizes, there are times that strict application of the formula seems unfair; the one man may not need nearly as much as he should be rewarded according to the formula, and the other may need more simply to survive. A similar sort of case would arise when a performer, desparate for engagements, signs a contract giving 90% of her earnings to an agent. Legally, the contract is just, but, Aristotle notes, it is not equitable. A judge will therefore have to violate the letter of the law, the formula, in order to insure genuine fairness. The community, however, will rarely raise an outcry; usually it will agree.

We can see the *sensus communis* operating in two ways here. First, it operates in the judge's sense that the formula is not fair. He is not appealing to his own private judgment, but to a communally shared sense of the good. Second, it operates in the community's recognition of the fairness of the decision, and later in the community's appeal to his precedent. In a similar vein, the sense of common good allows a minority

political party to be the *loyal* opposition, since it can be seen
as embodying the same communal values as the majority—
although it may disagree, often vehemently, about particulars.
Otherwise such a party would likely be regarded as merely
treasonous.

Since the *sensus communis* cannot be reduced to a formula,
it obviously cannot be taught as a formula. Yet as Aristotle
saw, it can be captured and exemplified by what the community regards as the best of its people, institutions and
books. There was a heavy emphasis on the humanities in the
classical liberal arts curriculum for precisely this reason. The
humanities lets us see these examples in history, literature and
the arts. As students read and discuss these ideas and events,
not only will they have the opportunity to see them face to
face but also to question them, and to question their own assumptions and prejudices. Of course, this only happens when
these courses are taught with an eye to the larger world, and
not simply as rehashes of theories about literary interpretation and historiography.

When the liberal arts curriculum is divided into departments each with its research specialty and own sphere of interest, then the curriculum itself, no longer unified, actively
works against the development of the whole person. Rather
than letting the student see the overarching moral sense of the
culture through the lens of, say, history, instead facts, dates
and method become all important. The case of one history
professor and his relationship to a student who was seeking
the "bigger picture" shows this. The professor became quite
upset because, he believed, the student was "not taking
enough notes," despite the fact that he was a superior student
and attentive in class. As a result the professor constantly
quizzed this student on particulars of the field during class
discussion, often ignoring the raised hands of other students.
Ironically, this professor saw himself as someone interested
in the "big picture" because he did once in a while admit comments—usually his own—about history's "relevancy." To

toss such a bone simply reinforced the fact that the broader discussion is only a side matter.

To develop the sense of a common good in which we actually participate is clearly something that can only happen through education. At first, this education takes place within our own family and the community in which we grow up. Later, in higher education, it occurs by broadening the student's cultural boundaries to include all of Western culture, not by the mere accumulation of facts but by allowing her to feel that she is a living part of it. She is a part of it when she is able to look at Solomon, Jesus, Socrates, Nietzche, Marx and Freud in making present judgments. She is a living part of it when she is able to draw upon these thinkers as sources of value which can help reform our community—when it needs reforming—along lines continuous with the past. With this sense of the larger community, she is not forever committed to starting over again with each new problem.

When the common good is not a goal in education, that good can be lost. In this regard education that merely cultivates or accepts social diversity, without trying to reach a higher cultural unity, may actually work against the development of the whole person. These are not abstract issues but ones at the heart of a great deal of contemporary discussion about education, as the following illustrations will show.

Recently many courses have been developed on a model of learning known as "critical thinking." In "critical thinking" a student who enters college able only to think in black and white terms is taught how to appreciate diversity—pluralism—and finally to think independently. The model itself is based on good empirical data and is often an immense help to teachers by giving them a way of understanding how their students actually learn. Where "critical thinking" may become a problem, however, is when it becomes an end in itself, that is, when the individual critical faculties are developed without the simultaneous development of roots. As

one professor of critical thinking admitted, Attila the Hun
could graduate from a critical thinking program, "as long as
he could see both sides of the issue." Attila, however, would
not have been given any standard by which to judge the issue.
This problem is not entirely unrecognized by theorists of
critical thinking and, in fact, there is a debate about whether
or not specific content is important in critical thinking
courses, since the critical faculty can be developed without
it. This may well suggest that someone who may think critically to a high degree is still not a whole person; she is merely skilled. Nevertheless the idea is often popular in liberal arts
colleges which have always sought to develop students' critical faculties; the problem remains that they may be substitut-
ing a mere part for the whole.

My second example is the frequent criticism of liberal arts
colleges and the liberal arts curriculum as a whole for being
"elitist," a criticism frequently voiced by John Dewey. It was
Dewey who argued that liberal arts education originally
belonged to an aristocratic class supported by slaves. Modern
democratic society, however, is very different; instead of
stressing linguistic skills and classics, therefore, education
ought to have the continuous application of science in jobs at
its heart. Anything less, Dewey claimed, would be un-
democratic. To be sure, he always realized the importance of
the past; unfortunately, as teachers have been increasingly
trained to find and develop individual talents which are socially useful, they, and increasingly their students, are unable
to articulate any sort of higher and broader social sense
beyond the merely utilitarian.

If elitism in education simply means giving diversions to
a leisured class, it is not valuable to a democracy. However,
in ridding ourselves of this unfortunate type of education we
must be careful that we do not lose the very studies that give
a democracy its sense of social coherence and vision. To be
rooted, it needs people who can stand above the pressure of
shortsighted need and popular opinion, people who can assess

the direction and goals of a society. These people do not need to constitute a superior economic class, but they do have to exist. A criticism of Allan Bloom's is helpful here. Bloom points out that it is the job of the state university to provide vocational education since the state has a major interest in seeing that particular functions within society are fulfilled. However, when this is the only educational goal, there is little possibility of our having a society that can decide whether or not those functions are even worthwhile. When no alternative is ever presented—the kinds of alternatives that private liberal arts colleges have traditionally offered—the demands and values of the immediate popular culture can only compete with each other; they cannot become part of a larger whole. The result is relativism, the common good understood at the level of the lowest common denominator. A people who are only trained to be cogs cannot see the larger whole, and in time democracy itself will lose its direction.

The communal sense needs to be stressed. We need to stress it because too often it goes unrecognized, yet it is vital to becoming a whole person. Yet there is also something about the whole person which is inescapably individual; as a whole person I am not simply a sheep in the fold of culture nor a mere scholar of tradition. Rather, I am a person who exercises judgment and so take responsibility for my own personal judgment. St. Paul recognizes this in his description of the body, insisting that each person within Christ's body has a particular role to play, which is not interchangeable with any other. Similarly Simone Weil recognized the importance of the individual when she argued that the transcendent basis of social morality is our individual obligations to other people. The community needs individuals of vision. It needs judges who can alter the letter of the law in order to discover its spirit. It needs individuals who can contribute to the common good.

Because we do have this need to develop individual judgment, it is clear that there was something wrong with the older style of pedagogy which simply inculcated lessons by rote. Much of what we know of the history of education indicates that this has always been the dominant style of teaching, and it is fortunate that we are losing it. Individual skills, initiative, the recognition of individual talents, the willingness to challenge authority—all these are necessary to the whole person. As one wise teacher noted, students also need to recognize what they are not good at. The whole person is not necessarily the universal scholar and athlete, but one who can make a unique contribution to the whole. Recognizing the limitations of our abilities is often essential for developing a sense of the whole in which our talents can be valuable.

One of the true joys of teaching in a liberal arts college that is not the size of a small city lies in being able to discover individual talents and aid them. It is wonderful to be able to attend to the shy freshman who seems bright enough, but appears to have no leadership ability, and then to watch her development over four years as she becomes, not necessarily the most popular person on campus, but a person of strong character who can speak quietly but wisely, who can lead by example.

Without such individuals, the body lacks both vision and richness. There is, however, an even more important reason. Although in order to be a whole person a student needs to feel himself part of a larger body and needs to draw life from it, the body also exists to support the individual. In this regard we have to recognize the limits of Paul's metaphor; we are not mere hands and feet, but full blooded people. The limits of the metaphor are especially evident with respect to an individual's relationship to institutions and traditions. In this regard Weil makes a telling point when she argues that institutions do not have a divine end, only people do. So we need to know what human ends really are in order to say in *which* body they should play a part. What are people to become by being a part of a larger whole?

Education must, on this count, ask the question Jacques Maritain posed forty five years ago: "What is the proper end of man towards which education is directed?"[4] For the Christian liberal arts colleges this question is crucial. While it is important for any liberal arts education to recognize the significance of the body of culture, in Christian liberal arts education the question, "Whose body?" must also arise in a very pointed way.

St. Paul claims: "For Christ is like a single body with its many limbs and organs, which, many as they are, together make up one body." If we simply follow Paul's analogy of the body we might reply to this question of "Whose body?" by saying it is Christ's body. However on the face of things this is no more than a slogan, one that might be very misleading if we simply took Paul's descriptions of the various parts of the body in I Corinthians 12 at face value. We might think, for example, that being a part of the whole would be to occupy some sort of preordained niche or function. Fortunately Paul gives a much fuller explanation of what it means to belong to Christ's body elsewhere in I Corinthians, an explanation that is helpful for understanding what the whole person might be in the light of a Christian form of education.

In the beginning of I Corinthians Paul tackles a problem that is dividing the Corinthian congregation. Apparently a number of the Corinthians have just received some slipshod instruction in philosophy that has led them to believe that they are full-fledged religious philosophers. As with all "half-education," this has unfortunate consequences. The half-educated Corinthians have begun to think themselves superior to everybody else in the congregation and to act that way. It is to this situation that Paul speaks, roundly criticizing them by pointing out that it is not philosophy that saves them. What is foolishness to the Greeks and a stumbling block to the Jews saves them—the absurdity of the cross. What matters most, Paul says, is something that simply cannot be expressed in

terms of philosophy and so they would be better off not trying
to be philosophers.

He is not saying, however, that people ought not to be educated. Paul himself was very well educated. What he is trying
to put across to the Corinthians is his belief that human
knowledge is limited and we ought not to depend upon it for
eternal things. Because of the very limitations of human
knowledge, eternal things themselves tend to look foolish;
human knowledge cannot see them as they really are.
Therefore Christians are, he claims, "foolish," not because
they are stupid, or ignorant, but because their wisdom is of a
different sort than what normally passes for wisdom in the
marketplace.

Paul does not simply leave his readers with this paradoxical idea, however. He goes on to say precisely what this "wisdom of the foolish" consists of, which is a "secret wisdom."
Paul points to himself as the exemplar of this wisdom: "We
have no power, but you are influential; you are celebrities and
we are nobody...we are treated as...the scum of the earth."(I
Corinthians 4:10,13 JB). It is something that has "put us
apostles at the end of [God's] parade," with little apparent
reward, to say nothing of the necessities for this life. Yet it is
not the contrary nature of his life as such that makes Paul
wise, it is the fact that he does it for the sake of the souls of
these very Corinthians who are causing him so much grief.
The secret wisdom that Paul teaches, therefore, is a
knowledge that enables him to serve others before himself,
just as Christ had done. This is what it means to be a part of
the body of Christ. The whole person, in Paul's eyes, is therefore not simply someone who is filling a niche, doing a job,
but the person who draws sustenance from Christ's body and
who uses it for the good of others, that they may also be
nourished by God. In serving the body they fulfill themselves;
the body, in turn, enables them to realize their own individual
ends.

Paul gives a clear answer to the question, "Whose body?" and he can define pretty accurately who belongs to it. Yet he has also left a major question for all Christian education since the time he wrote I Corinthians, and that question is the degree to which Christians might also belong to the larger body of the culture.

One answer has been that of sectarianism, which forcefully claims that the wisdom of the foolish and the wisdom of human culture are mutually exclusive. It is interesting to note that when Tertullian formulated his famous question, "What does Athens have to do with Jerusalem?" he had this idea in mind. Within the context of that question, Tertullian was not so much worried about philosophy as such (he was a good classical philosopher himself) but of allowing Christian students to participate in Roman education. This parallel with modern fundamentalism is striking. Tertullian argued that since Roman education was mainly taught through the use of pagan myths, Christians ought to avoid it as much as they possibly could. They belonged to the body of Christ and so should separate themselves from the body of Roman and Greek culture, becoming a separate culture of their own.

Sectarianism, however, has not been the only answer to this question. The answer that has in fact won out is quite different, and it is exemplified by numerous ancient writers such as Justin Martyr, Clement of Alexandria and Augustine, all of whom used the best of Greco-Roman culture to Christian advantage. If one dares to find a common understanding of what it means to be Christ's body in these writers, it is one that is based on the Incarnation. As orthodox theology has always understood, Christ's body was not a spiritual thing, but a body just like any other human body; so too, he also had a fully human mind that was limited to understanding what his religion and culture could teach him. But since he was also God, he put that body to ends that were not limited by his culture, but by God alone. If one uses this understanding of the

Incarnation as a metaphor for the Christian education's relation to culture, it is this: to belong to Christ's body does not
mean to be outside the body of culture, but to use it for Christian ends, the service of others, and to inform it with God's
purposes. It may also mean to resist all unworthy ends.

If we try to describe the Christian understanding of the
whole person, then, we describe a person who fully embodies
a sense of the common good that includes the broader culture,
but is not limited to it. For her ends are informed by something more ultimate and her talents developed in accordance
with those ends. She draws life and inspiration from her culture, but her ultimate source of light would come from God.
Her service to her community would be her witness to the
fullness of life.

In many ways this ideal of the whole person is one that has
always been attempted by the Christian liberal arts. It tries to
give not only a social and secular education, but also valid alternatives for how we are to live. This search for alternatives
has always been a struggle, since a culture embodies so many
diverse elements and not all of them are equally worthy. At
the present moment it may be necessary for us to acknowledge that a shortsighted popular and material culture prevails
in education. Yet we should not overdo this. The problems of
the present are not exactly the same problems that Tertullian
faced when he confronted a culture which, despite its
worthwhile elements, was entirely pagan. For the culture in
which we now live is one that has been greatly influenced by
Christianity, even if there are other elements existing
alongside. In this regard the broader culture of the West can
be a help to religious education, even if, as T.S. Eliot quipped,
"bishops are a part of English culture, and horses and dogs
are a part of English religion."[5] The sectarian answer is a poor
one, since for the twentieth century person the withdrawal
from the larger culture may turn out to be a form of uprooting. It is in this regard that the Christian liberal arts colleges
have an important part to play in the formation of the whole

Christian person, since they alone offer the opportunity of in-
stilling a sense both of the broader culture and of the distinct-
ly Christian ends to which the culture might be put. T.S. Eliot
also remarked: "As the world at large becomes more completely secularized, the need becomes more urgent that
professedly Christian people should have a Christian education, which should be an education both for this world and for
the life of prayer in this world."[6]

What is necessary to discover is how that "Christian"
education Eliot sought might look. How might it be an
education in faith, an education that fits us for the body of
Christ, as well as an education of intellectual freedom and
responsibility?

Chapter Three

Goodbye Mr. Chips

If we were to imagine a college in which its members put each other's welfare before their own, we might imagine it staffed by faculty members who resemble the hero of James Hilton's *Goodbye Mr. Chips.* "Chips" was a man who had given his life and loyalty to Brookfield, "a good school of the second rank." He remembered every boy he ever taught. He also had a wonderful sense of proportion, ranging from his well-worn ways of teaching Latin to his equally worn academic gown. Without a doubt, teachers such as Chips are a gift from God in their ability to care. However, it is not very realistic to expect we who teach will be like that any more that we can expect our parents to be what we remember from "Father Knows Best." Nor would we want to be like Chips in every way: while quaintness and routine may be appropriate to teaching Latin to fourth form boys, it is rarely so for college professors. A Chips can very easily be a man whose own education has stopped years ago. We might well recall that Chips himself "in any social or academic sense, was just as respect able, but no more brilliant, than Brookfield itself."

The primary job of a professor is to teach and to teach well. Good will towards students and subject matter is not enough, even when it is infectious. This point was emphasized in a conversation I once heard between a visiting scholar and a colleague of mine. The visitor recalled a time when, as a junior faculty member, he was assigned to teach one of his department's large introductory courses in an area where he had only rudimentary knowledge. His semester, he laughed, consisted of staying half an hour ahead of his students. To his surprise, he added, few of his courses had ever been so well received by his students. At that point my colleague broke in with the suggestion that the course was exciting because the man was conveying his own excitement of learning. Since virtually all of us who were listening to this exchange had had the same experience, we initially agreed. The visitor, however, had grave doubts about the suggestion. For, he pointed out, he was not very sure that he had really given them anything that they *should* have been excited about; he may only have succeeded in exciting them to a superficial grasp of the subject and in encouraging them to seek the same thing in other courses. Teaching does not have to be dry nor does it have to be entertaining; it does have to be honest.

What the Christian liberal arts requires from a faculty member is somebody intellectually deeper than a Mr. Chips. Yet it also needs professors who have something more than competence in a field. It needs people who care, people who understand that the idea of the "whole person" is more than a metaphor for a person who has integrated all of his talents well. But it also needs scholars who understand that this wholeness also includes a student's integration into the whole of a much larger body. Without this larger sense of the whole, one ends up with, at best, a skilled person whose relationship to others is often ambiguous. Teachers who have a sense that humans are meant for communion with God and service to others, who can use that sense in giving a truly human education, are crucial.

Two things are essential to the Christian liberal arts: a sense of coherence and ultimacy pervading the entire curriculum, and a sense of the real ends of education. Subject matter not only needs to be taught, but placed in a moral context, the context of good and evil. In part this context must be established by the curriculum; its actual success, however,

depends upon teachers who not only teach a subject matter
thoroughly, but also can place it in the light of something
more ultimate. This does not mean biologists ought necessarily to confront students about the morality of Darwinism
while they are trying to count generations of fruitflies. It does
mean that biologists ought to make themselves aware of the
larger moral and theological context of knowledge and allow
it to infuse its spirit into their teaching. Since science students
are virtually ignorant of both the philosophy and history of
science—areas in which they can establish bridges to the
humanities—they should be made aware of these fields and
the questions they raise for doing science. It would also be
helpful to hold something as simple as an occasional discussion of science's ultimate justification. Students ought in the
end to see the difference between taking biology because it
leads to medical school and in taking it because knowing and
understanding the physical processes of life is valuable
knowledge. Teachers are crucial for understanding this difference both in how they teach and how they use their own
knowledge—whether they use it to maintain a job or as a
means toward living a whole life.

   In this regard Mr. Chips is not entirely to be dismissed. In
some antiquated way he does show us that teaching calls for
something more than intellectual brilliance. Teaching needs
to be an activity of the whole person, even if it is not all that
a person does. A teacher who is using her knowledge as a
means toward a whole life cannot simply confine her contributions to the classroom. In order to be effective, she really
ought to contribute and support the social and religious life
of the campus. Just as a teacher who proclaims the ideal of
the liberal arts but refuses ever to venture outside his field is
contradicting his own teaching, so too a teacher who talks
about belonging to a larger body but does not participate in it
is hypocritical. Teachers and administrators who advertise a
school as belonging to the Christian liberal arts tradition, but
regularly schedule meetings during the open hour reserved

for chapel, make it quite clear to the students that there are concerns more important than worship. Students are very aware of these messages and easily point to them to defend their own non-participation.

The participation of teachers in community life, however, is more than avoiding the appearance of hypocrisy or setting an example. It also needs to take place in areas of which students are rarely aware, namely in the deliberations which determine the academic and social structure of a college. Many professors are content to leave their contributions in the classroom simply because the politics of changing institutional structures are so unrewarding and discouraging, while the egos involved are so large. More than one college has a faculty which complains bitterly about the administration and students over coffee cups, but is always in a hurry to get the monthly faculty meeting over by dinner time. Yet since the overall community is so crucial to the learning of the whole person, and since it is a larger community still for which we are trying to educate students, we cannot in good conscience avoid such politics. These politics need vision and courage. They also need people who can unselfishly look to a greater good instead of protecting private turf, and who can withstand pressures, including administrative ones, to become more "realistic" by becoming more utilitarian.

It would be platitudinous simply to recommend vision, courage and a greater good without giving these notions some reality and weight. Education takes place in a very large context, not only in schools, but also in families, on the street, and in churches. Each place of education makes a contribution to the shaping of the overall person and one ought not to expect that anybody will receive all of her education in any one place. Educational attempts in one situation can also be undermined by another. For example, it is popular to blame schools for the ignorance of school children; however, if they are spending most of their time at home watching television without much parental supervision, schools are hardly the sole problem with the child's education. Similarly, studies on Christian education have shown that Sunday schools bring children to an awareness of the Christian faith only when such efforts parallel those at home. For those children whose parents merely drop them off at Sunday school and who then pick them up afterwards without going to church themselves, there will be little in that one hour on Sunday morning that is likely to take hold in their lives.

It is important to understand this larger context of education when teaching because we are not solely responsible for the formation of the whole person. This does not excuse whatever failures may occur; it is to observe carefully that when discussing the form of education we are trying to present, including that of the Christian liberal arts, we are discussing only one part. In order to discuss the Christian liberal arts intelligently we need to understand what specific role it plays and ought to play in the formation of the whole person. This will also allow us to see better, in a later chapter, the role that the church plays, for the Christian liberal arts school is not the same thing as an advanced Sunday school.

What is the the role of teachers in educating the whole person? Primarily it is an intellectual role in both the larger culture and the church. As is fairly obvious, colleges are institutions that have concentrated almost their entire energies on the development of the intellect and it is good that they have. Few people can develop even a very shallow knowledge of science, literature, psychology or any other field of knowledge simply by drawing upon the resources at their command. Often colleges and universities are accused of being "ivory towers;" that, however, is precisely what they ought to be. Without a time away from the pressing demands of commerce one is going to be distracted so many times and so many ways that any sort of progress is impossible. In order to develop the intellect well, one has to make a concentrated effort. That is exactly what colleges are for.

It is far too simple, however, to say that colleges have the role of developing the "intellectual" side of the whole person—as if it could be developed in isolation. Instead, the intellect, just as any other part of a person, plays an organic role, contributing and drawing from the whole. For this reason, we need to teach with an eye to the intellect's part in the whole, educating students in those areas that are important to a culture. An education in science, for example, is absolutely essential to any student in the twentieth century, as is an education in the principles of democracy. It is equally important to Christianity that Christian students be given an education in matters essential to Christianity. By giving this education we do not necessarily produce in every case scientists, politicians or theologians; we do hope to produce people who do not regard technology as an unfathomable mystery on the order of magic, or who regard politicians as the high priests of an unseen power that cannot be questioned. We also hope to produce people who are capable of scientific judgment when dealing with empirical questions in their own lives and who are capable of participating in the democratic process. And we hope to produce a person to whom the tradition and history of Christianity is not completely foreign.

The intellectual education of the whole person, however, is still more than developing expertise in science, political theory or theology, even if they are each important for the continuation and advancement of the culture. We also need to bring a student to a deeper awareness of the culture as a whole; for this reason the traditional attempt of the liberal arts to educate a person's mind broadly is important. The *sensus communis* so important to being a whole person is not, as it were, a platonic idea that lurks in its entirety behind different cultural disguises—literary, scientific, musical and the like. Rather, its wholeness is contained in the ensemble of individual cultural achievements; it cannot be understood or appreciated apart from them. Just as we cannot understand

Plato by concentrating on his theory of forms and ignoring
his ideas on art, politics and ethics, or understand the faith
Jesus inspired in the disciples by reading only a single gospel,
so too we cannot understand the unity of our culture without
seeing it in its many parts. Whatever communal sense that exists among us should be reflected in the intellectual training
of students.

Because intellectual development cannot be divorced from
moral development a liberal education is also a moral education. In fact, if a person is to participate fully and creatively
within the body of culture, his education must be moral from
beginning to end. This may seem paradoxical, but for teachers
to develop and train the intellect well, we must also train it
to understand that all human thought and action takes place
within a moral context. We are able to train scientists to
produce weapons of apocalyptic force; we have not done a
very good job of giving them any way to see the gravity of
the task, as Oppenheimer complained after the Manhattan
Project on which he had worked issued in Hiroshima and
Nagasaki. Thinking directs our actions and our actions are
always subject to moral assessment. Therefore whatever
teaching of the intellect we do needs to be done with an acute
awareness of moral ends.

Two of Christianity's greatest educators were St. Augustine and John Henry Newman. Both can shed important light
on this question of the relationship between the training of
the intellect and ultimate moral ends.

At the beginning of his treatise *On Christian Teaching*,
Augustine introduces a distinction that applies to all we do
and have. Everything, he notes, is either to be used for something else or is to be enjoyed for itself. The overriding question in life, therefore, is to determine what is to be enjoyed
for itself and what is useful for discovering and enjoying it.
Now for Augustine there is only one thing that is to be fully
enjoyed for itself—God. Everything else, no matter how important we think it is—including the Bible—is to be used to

bring oneself to the enjoyment of God. So it is important to decide how to order useful things for approaching God; Augustine claims that the Bible is chief among these. Yet as he points out, the Bible is of no help to us if we cannot read it and understand it. Education of all kinds is essential. We need education not only so that we may learn to decipher the words of the Bible but also so that we may know what they mean and to what they refer. If we knew nothing about astronomy, for example, we would have little appreciation of the many literal and figurative expressions that involve the stars. For these reasons, Augustine thinks we need a education that includes grammar, logic and rhetoric as well as various sciences—in short, we need to go through the entire cycle of the classical liberal arts.

Augustine's educational system was primarily directed towards interpreting the Bible, especially allegorically. There is, however, a major difference between him and the modern fundamentalists who profess to teach only what is in the Bible. The latter have tended to hold much the same attitude to secular knowledge as the Muslim caliph who burned the great ancient library at Alexandria did. The caliph justified his barbarity on the grounds that everything in the library that was true was already in the Koran and therefore redundant, or it was false and deserved to be burned. In Augustine's system, on the other hand, everything that is true, when properly ordered, is useful for attaining the vision of God. This was certainly how the later medieval thinkers understood him. But this ultimately means, as was well recognized, that all truth has a moral and spiritual context and the effectiveness of any truth depends upon recognizing that context. The education of the mind must be understood in light of its ultimate end.

Newman presents a somewhat different case than Augustine, and over the course of his life offered two divergent views of what education was to do. The story of Newman's involvement with education is one that began when he was a tutor at Oriel College in Oxford University during the 1830's.

Oxford was just beginning to show signs at that time of awaking from an intellectual slumber during which it had become, in today's vernacular, a party school for the rich, and Newman was determined to shape it according to proper principles when it did awake.

Now one of the particular ways that he did this was to reconceive the role of tutor as he believed it had originally been established in the middle ages when Oxford was founded. Rather than simply seeing tutors as some sort of intellectual coach, for Newman they also fulfilled a spiritual function. At the time, considering that most of Oxford's tutors were clergymen in the Church of England, this view should not have seemed too far-fetched—although a number of tutors apparently thought so.

Newman had a particular reason for insisting that the tutors fulfil this spiritual office. At a time when Oxford was full of reform schemes for establishing new systems of education, Newman declared "that the difference between this or that system is as nothing compared with the effects of the human will upon them, that till the will be changed from evil to good, the difference of the results between two given systems will be imperceptible." In short, Newman saw the goal of education as correcting and directing the will. One could change the mechanics all one wanted, but until one changed the character of the people who lived within the system, one had done nothing. The tutors, therefore, were to direct a good part of their energy to the moral improvement of their students— while still paying attention to their minds, so that their students would not become narrow and bigoted.

Thirty years after the Oxford reform Newman, now converted to Roman Catholicism, got another chance to put his educational ideals into practice when he was called upon to found the Catholic University in Dublin and serve as its first president. As part of those duties he delivered the set of lectures that has subsequently come down to us as *The Idea of a University*, one of the truly great works in the philosophy of education. It is interesting to note the change that thirty years had wrought. For there Newman declared not that the chief aspect of education is education of the will, but rather the prime focus of education is *intellectual*. To be sure, he still argued that the university should still teach the morals and the doctrines of the Christian faith, but he did not think that the university could or should teach students to believe or practice them. That is the function of the church, and the university could not be expected to fill the function of a church.

As a sidelight it might be noted that very few of the faculty that Newman hired in Dublin were clergy.

What brought about this change? It would appear that Newman in his most developed thought had come to a position that we today hold as self-evident; namely, education is a matter of free intellect and colleges have no business directing students in what they must believe and practice. In fact, with the exception of a few fundamentalist universities where doctrinal and moral expectations are still maintained with some rigor, Newman's position may even be called universal.

I have not brought up Newman simply to point out that he thought the same about education as we do. The fact of the matter is that even at the end he didn't see it as we do now. It is precisely in where he differs from us that we have something to learn from him.

For despite his assertions when founding the Catholic University of Dublin, Newman never gave up on his position that the education of the will is important. Indeed, he always thought that it is the most important education we can receive. If God reveals truth, and if our moral life is a matter of obeying God, then whether we choose to believe God and to obey God's will is clearly the most important aspect of our lives. Whatever opinions our intellect toys with are really secondary to the life we actually lead.

Where Newman had changed since his Oxford days was not in the way he saw the education of the will, but in the way he viewed the university's role in that education. To be sure, the university is not to expect compliance with specific doctrinal and moral standards, but the education it gives to the intellect is, nevertheless, important to how we finally choose to act. By giving the intellect free rein, investigating freely where curiosity leads it and never fearing truth (for Newman the truths of Christianity are never contradicted by any other truth, including the scientific truths of Darwin) when we consent to follow God's will, we will do so freely and with joy. A world that we can apprehend as friendly to our minds and wills, as good and beautiful, is a world that we can consent to as part of God's good intention. So our consent is not a matter of a grudging surrender to what is merely a stronger will, but an occasion of joy and enthusiasm that forever seeks wider expression.

Newman's ideas on education—its goals and means—are important for us to understand when we try to relate the training of the intellect to moral ends. We may already agree with him that a liberal arts education is meant to free the intellect and make it feel at home in the world. What we do not understand and so can learn from Newman is responsibility. This freedom is one that has to be used for a higher goal, namely, the education of our wills. It determines how we live our lives—with grace and gratitude, or not. The question of how we live is the very basis of a Christian liberal arts education; both administration and faculty ought explicitly to recognize it as such. What we are after is not, in Newman's terms, "mere philosophy," but a good life, one that can find and love God's purpose in the world.

It is a life of purpose that we ought to be after, and whatever knowledge we hand out ought to be somehow useful in that life. What we are educating our students *for*, then, is to be able to choose that life. Although we cannot expect rigorous adherence to moral and doctrinal systems and still remain a school, we also cannot ignore or forget that what and why we teach is, ultimately, so that a student may shape her life well.

Because we are dealing with some of the deepest parts of students' lives, we cannot take either what we teach or how we teach casually. Students rarely recognize at once the ultimate value of what they learn and often in introductory courses do not hesitate to show that they think it is irrelevant. As a result many professors tailor these courses to their perception of student abilities. Rather than asking poor writers to write more, or ignorant students to read more, they give only as much as they think students can take. Far from being good teaching, this is thinly disguised cynicism. Good teaching involves at least two major elements: subject matter that feeds the serious inner needs of students and an explicit recognition of the relationship of education to the knowledge of good and evil.

The importance of subject matter can perhaps best be seen by taking a rare case in American liberal arts education where the content of teaching has been a prime curricular issue. I have in mind the "Great Books" curriculum begun by Mortimer Adler at the University of Chicago in the 1930s and best exemplified nowadays by St. John's College of Annapolis and Santa Fe. Students are given virtually no choice in the courses they take; instead, they are served a common menu of something over one hundred "great books" of western culture, beginning with Homer in their freshman year and ending with Einstein, Heidegger and Wittgenstein. The books are taught in seminar style classes that are divided into language, laboratory, mathematics and music "tutorials" along with a twice weekly seminar on large works of literature and philosophy. This curriculum may not be one that could or should be instituted universally, but it has a number of points in its favor.

In the first place, this curriculum can introduce the student at some depth to the *sensus communis* of western culture, both in its broad common aspects and also, by comparison, to its contemporary aspects. If it does nothing else, at least a student becomes aware of the broad range of western culture. These books in many ways *are* the tradition of western culture. As Hans-Georg Gadamer in his major work on the humanities has observed, "Literature is a function of intellectual preservation and tradition, and therefore brings its hidden history into every age."[7] Moreover, such a curriculum also keeps students from learning by rote; whatever formulae they come away from it with are ones they have had to discover themselves. They will have the chance not only to find out what Descartes and Freud actually said, but also to see what questions are common to both. They will be forced to come to grips with other great thinkers on such questions as "What is the good?" Whatever they come to think about any idea will at some point involve a larger moral question.

Such a curriculum, however, does more than raise abstract questions about the good. By deliberately choosing the "best" books, it exemplifies them. The authors of these books, unlike the writers of textbooks, are not merely reporting opinions but forming them just as the students are expected to do. In this way, it is no exaggeration to claim that the books themselves are the real teachers. In fact, in an honest but witty piece of advertising, St. John's claims: "Next year the following teachers will return to St. Johns—Plato, Aristotle, Augustine, Freud, Darwin. . . ." They are teachers, however, which the students are expected to question as critically as they themselves are questioned.

When the founders of the St. John's program established the criteria for "great books" they not only included timelessness and and artistic excellence, but insisted that these books raise the persistent unanswerable questions of the human mind. They also sought books which have the "greatest number of alternative, independent and consistent interpretations." They were seeking not ambiguous books, but universal ones, requiring multiple interpretations just as the

New Testament requires four gospels to show the universality of Jesus' appeal. What they expected of the books was exactly what they expected of students and teachers—people who strive for depth without rigidity. A person who can both speak to and listen to many different people is liberally educated. This ideal has been pushed so far at St. John's that the tutors are required to teach in all areas of the curriculum. This is a far cry from many other liberal arts colleges that cannot staff interdisciplinary courses because nobody will teach outside his field—despite the insistence that students be broadly educated.

When students work with foundational texts, these texts cease being historical museum pieces. They become the opportunity for actually participating in the culture. As a student seriously wrestles with an Aristotle or a Nietzche, she makes him a part of her life and the lives she touches. But she also becomes a part of the culture herself. Far from merely accepting certain works as great, she becomes part of the reason why they are great. Although any group of books designed for four years of under graduate education is necessarily limited, it cannot be arbitrary; an arbitrary curriculum could not survive. The desire to know can only be fulfilled by knowing.The ability of students, therefore, to make something of certain books in their lives and throughout the course of their lives is an important part of cultural activity.

Each spring I teach a course in the New Testament. Except for one brief book used for only two weeks at the beginning of the semester, the only textbook required is the New Testament itself. The point of the course is, naturally, to enable students to read the New Testament for themselves and to ease their difficulties in understanding it. Yet each year's round of course evaluations inevitably contains as an answer to the question, "How useful are the texts assigned?": "Useful as a supplement to the lectures." What those comments reveal is a mind set that views courses and their content as strictly a matter of information, a set body of material that exists outside the mind. Teaching and learning is the process of depositing the New Testament in the mind as if it were a foreign substance. Assuming it does get deposited sooner or later, the student and the material still remain foreign to each other. Christianity itself remains foreign, and since such students undoubtedly see the rest of the education in the same way, so does virtually all of their heritage.

The opportunity to participate in the best of culture has particular spiritual benefits. It gives students a sense of place and belonging within the world. When Simone Weil argued that one of our deepest needs is for roots she said that we cannot reach great spiritual depths when we feel that we don't belong. Without a sense of belonging to something larger and more ultimate, which our cultural heritage helps us to do, the world appears chaotic. Without a sense of purpose, the very notion of being a whole person seems vacuous. One cannot have a coherent life in an incoherent world. I will take up in the next chapter the importance for a liberal arts education to give an overall sense of purpose; for now it is enough to say that the capacity that education gives us of participating in something greater than ourselves is crucial to developing that sense.

If the content of the courses we teach is critical for establishing the ultimate moral context of education, so is its understanding of good and evil. Yet it is more commonly as sumed that objective intellectual matters are morally neutral—an assumption that is in good part due to modern science, which claims such a neutrality. Many philosophers of science and scientists dispute this, yet most academic disciplines still assume it—just as people do at cocktail parties. Everybody seems to take as established beyond the shadow of a doubt some hard-and-fast distinction between hard objective facts and soft subjective values. For example, if we make a controversial statement, it follows that someone will ask us, "Is that a fact, or only a value judgment?" Notice the use of the word "only." This distinction is a fiction. Our facts and values are intertwined in very important ways, and we cannot pretend to be educating the whole person unless we make that explicit.

The Harvard philosopher Hilary Putnam gives an example of how facts and values are interconnected. Imagine, he says, a nation of people who are "super-utilitarians." They believe that any act that will increase utility by even the slightest amount ought to be carried out since it increases the amount of good in society. Since lying will in many cases—perhaps too many, as we all know—increase utility, these people will in time come to be proficient liars. They will even see lying as their moral duty. So over the course of time what these people will regard as facts will differ considerably from what we regard as facts. But, like us, they will also use the "facts" at their disposal to back up their moral judgments. In time there will be no arguing with them, for they will end up inhabiting a world entirely different from ours. Of course, the world won't really be different for them, but it will look different and all because they place a value on lying.

Facts and values cannot be separated and it is a myth to think they can. Yet this lays a responsibility upon us as members of the academic profession; it means that we need to examine our values and our facts very carefully to discover what they are, and to develop our values in order to do our jobs. In educating the whole person such a discovery is crucial. I don't suppose that this means we will spend a lot of time in math classes discussing the morality of the quadratic equation, but it might not be a bad idea once in awhile to discuss what mathematics tells us about truth, and how truth is necessary to human flourishing. Yet that doesn't happen often, even in the humanities.

C.S. Lewis opens his little book on education, *The Abolition of Man*, by citing a grammar textbook which he had recently received as a complimentary copy. The book, Lewis

notes, discusses a passage in Samuel Coleridge where two
men before a waterfall argue whether the sight is "pretty" or
"sublime." The textbook has this to say: "When the one said
the sight was sublime he actually was saying 'I have feelings
associated in my mind with the word "sublime," or shortly, I
have sublime feelings.'" It then adds: "We appear to be saying
something very important about something; and actually we
are only saying something about our own feelings."

Lewis points out that these comments are ridiculous, for
we do not have "sublime feelings" in front of the sublime; we
have feelings of reverence and awe. Similarly, when we say
that somebody is contemptible, we are certainly not saying
that *we* are having contemptible feelings. Yet the problem
with the book, Lewis says, is not the appearance of a mistake
that leads to a bizarre claim, but rather that the textbook is
promoting a piece of bad philosophy and doing so under the
guise of grammatical principles. That, at least, is bad education; it worsens, however, when that covert philosophy
actually wars in the end with true education.

There are a number of reasons for agreeing with Lewis that
the textbook is promoting bad philosophy and bad education.
On the one hand, it subtly informs us that values are strictly
a matter of feeling, and therefore probably not very important. On the other hand, it also hides this controversial item
under the guise of what to a student is supposed to be a non-
controversial grammatical principle. Just at the time the
students are seeking lasting values, they receive the not-so-
subtle message that there really aren't any. Any education that
tries to look at the difference between good and evil, at moral
struggle, is going to be undermined to the point that it appears
ludicrous.

The point of this example is not that there are bad textbooks
out there—every teacher knows that perfectly well—but that
the books we put into their hands and the ideas we put into
their heads are going to have something to do with good and
evil. Nothing is exempt. Nevertheless even parents, who have

a major duty to give their children values and structure, are told assuredly by the "experts" responsible for the latest vogue in child-rearing—"parent effectiveness training—that they should avoid doing exactly that. The social critic Christopher Lasch has ironically summarized the movement: "Objective statements should be excluded from discourse with the child, according to this reasoning, in the first place because no one can argue rationally about beliefs and in the second place because statements about reality convey ethical judgments and therefore arouse strong emotions."[8] Yet Lasch points out that when we do not give children a sense of value and reality, but merely affirm their feelings," all of which are to be treated as "legitimate," we make our children vulnerable to manipulation and even to the savage retribution of their own psychic processes.

Northrop Frye also has something to say about values and information:

> Several best-selling books lately have been telling us how the most advanced societies of our time, that is to say our own, are moving from an industry-based to an information-based form of social organization. This thesis doubtless appeals strongly to a middle management who would rather issue memoranda than produce goods at competitive prices. But what is really curious about such books is the conception of information involved. Surely everyone knows that information is not a placid river of self explanatory facts; it comes to us prepackaged in ideological containers, and many of these containers have been constructed by professional liars. There is such a thing, of course as a genuine information explosion, but even in the most benevolent forms of acquiring information, such as research in the arts and sciences, most of the work involved consists in extricating oneself from a web of misinformation, after which the researcher hands over to posterity

what he has put together, with *its* quota of mistakes and prejudices.[9]

Even at their most "objective," what a student gets out of his studies comes down to his being able to distinguish lies from truth. What he passes on will depend on his dedication to being truthful, just as what he heard in the first place depended on his teacher's truthfulness. If you don't think this is really such a large moral matter, try the rather sobering fantasy of a world being run by the students whom you have taught, using the techniques that you have taught them. In fact, the experiment has already been tried. One Wisconsin college decided to use its endowment in order to fund student loans and then nearly went bankrupt when a large number of its graduates failed to pay off the loans, despite their ability to do so.

It is because of this intertwining of facts and values, as well as the larger moral context of education, that the liberal arts are regaining a great deal of respect in education these days. The more or less unified curriculum of the liberal arts and its traditional interest in the whole person allows it to treat matters of value better than most forms of education. So it is common to find many liberal arts colleges including in their catalogues statements about how they help to develop a student's "sense of values." Nevertheless we should be very careful when trying to understand what it means to develop a student's sense of values. There is often a great deal of confusion about this matter. For example, many teachers and schools talk about education being a matter of "values clarification." While it is certainly a good thing to be clear about the values one holds, if education is no more than a matter of clarifying values it is not much really different than psychoanalysis or plastic surgery. The analyst or surgeon will help you to whatever sort of personality or nose you might like; they might even help you clarify your preferences.

Moral or aesthetic judgments, however, are no real concern of theirs.

Thus education is in the end a matter of teaching the discernment of good and evil and so guiding students' physical, intellectual, emotional and spiritual choices accordingly. This is a strong statement and a huge responsibility. Unfortunately all of us have seen too often the terrible mistakes that have been made in the name of goodness. It is because of those mistakes that we sometimes prefer the more modest approach of simply trying to clarify values; then, at least, we cannot be accused of hypocrisy. But this more modest approach will not work, for the simple reason that we are already involved in teaching about real good and evil. Students are not waiting to make decisions about their values; they are acting on the values they already have, just as the rest of the world does. They are also modifying those values, even if imperceptibly, in accord with what they have heard from their teachers. In that case, we are involved in their moral education anyhow and we need to do it well.

But let us understand that teaching students about the difference between good and evil does not mean that we ought to be zealots and fanatics, imposing in whatever way we can our values upon others. Fanaticism is surely on the darker side of the division of good and evil. What it does mean is that students ought to be treated as teachers should be teaching themselves—an intellectual golden rule, I suppose. We need to look deep inside ourselves to see whether we are following convenience or justice, truth or pedantry, nonsense or profundity. Students must be taught to do the same.

We ought to deal with our students, for example, in a Socratic manner—but by that I do not mean the television law school version of the "Socratic method," where a student is badgered and bullied into giving a predetermined answer. I mean the method Socrates actually used. Socrates first listened to his conversational partner and then tried to get *him* to draw out the consequences of his position. If those consequences were good, Socrates was willing to be convinced. If they weren't, well, then, Socrates had just done the fellow a favor by letting him understand that. But in any case Socrates was a fellow seeker. It is in just such a manner that we have to teach people self-examination and engage in it ourselves.

The question remains, self-examination for what? There are a number of important values that need to be stressed in education. First, in the best tradition of the west, there is the value of truth and its relation to beauty. For the Greeks, one was a mark of the other and that interrelation was a major basis of their culture, as it should be of ours. The value of community is also essential—it is essential not only to those who are taught, but to those who teach. In all individual disciplines, we must understand ourselves as engaged in a common enterprise and a common dialogue. No discipline or department can afford to be an isolated fiefdom, for once it becomes that then there is no good to be held in common.

We also need to stress the value of that reasonableness which is sometimes called openness, a value that flows from and into the values of community, truth and an all embracing good. Openness is not, however, mere tolerance, what George Bernard Shaw called the virtue of the person who believes nothing. Rather it is the value of realizing the limitations of one's own position and the need to seek more deeply for what is lasting. Kant once noted the necessity of this reasonableness, this openness, for liquidating the doubt that plagues every honest commitment to an intellectual position: "The root of these disturbances, which lie deep in the nature of human reason, must be removed. But how can we do so, unless we give it freedom, nay nourishment, to send out its shoots so that it may discover itself to our eyes and that it may then be entirely destroyed?...We have nothing to fear, but much to hope for; namely, that we may gain for our selves a possession which can never be contested."[10]

Yet in the end self-examination, the values of truth, beauty, community and reasonableness also need a standard. What is it? It is one that the western tradition has often shared with Christianity, but one on which Christianity remains adamant. It is the standard that any teacher ought to recognize if it really makes a difference to her that students know the difference between good and evil. It is teaching others because it is good for *them*, because *they* need to know the difference between good and evil. It is the standard of giving to others. That is the richest standard of all, for it is God's own. Not only did he give up a Son that we might know good and evil and be able to follow the good, he did so that we might do the same for others. To invoke the notion of sacred duty sounds old-fashioned, but since education has to do with the inner lives of others, in the end it may be the best way of putting it.

Chapter Four

Queen of the Sciences?

In recent years there has been an extensive wave of curricular changes sweeping American colleges and universities. Unlike the changes of the 1960's, however, this wave of changes has not been particularly innovative; instead, educators have set it in motion in order to regain a sense of coherence that many colleges fear they have lost. One dean typically confessed: "We had to restore some coherence to the curriculum. We had too many superficial survey courses. Getting a degree was like filling in a Green Stamp book."

Everybody wants to be thought coherent; the alternative is unthinkable. But what exactly is the problem of coherence in an educational curriculum? In the first place, without it one's studies and therefore one's knowledge of the world will not interrelate, except by accident. Second, a lack of coherence also means a failure to posit any sort of larger context—any sort of overarching purpose—to life. This has enormous moral and religious implications; by their very nature morality and religion are one part, if not the whole of, that larger context. The inability to imagine a larger context may well be an inability to think morally or religiously, except in a piecemeal way. Even when there is respect for both learning and the knowledge that is essential for a whole life, that is not enough. Without coherence, it is difficult to imagine learning as communal or as leading to communal life; when knowledge is fragmented it is no longer shared.

Moreover this incoherence may also have larger consequences, which affect the whole of society. Loss of a sense of overarching purpose in higher education signals a further loss and direction and purpose in the thinking of college graduates. So it is likely that short-term goals without long-range vision will come to dominate a society's daily life. This is not even a theoretical possibility, but the often-heard complaint of experienced American businessmen about their younger colleagues, which has caused them a great deal of concern for the future of American business.

Concern for coherence has not merely been confined to college and university education. In his book *Theologia*, Edward Farley raises it for theological education as well. His criticisms and suggestions parallel many that might also be made about liberal arts education. Theological education, Farley argues, has lost *theologia*—the knowledge of God that is wisdom rather than the mastery of a specialized discipline—as its goal and unity. Such education is instead determined by the tasks of the professional clergy, with the result that theology is thought of as part of the functional tasks of ministry.

The problem is further compounded, Farley contends, by the fact that the curriculum of most theological education is divided into discrete fields and departments. These fields are usually determined by scholarly methodology and not by any broader view of how they might contribute to the formation of a mind imbued with the wisdom of God. Virtually all of these fields, with the exception of practical theology, are then regarded by seminarians and ministers as simply theoretical—so largely irrelevant to their tasks. Farley's judgment is confirmed by an observation of Joseph Sittler, the eminent Lutheran theologian, who notes that in his many years of preaching as a guest minister, he has always investigated the resident pastor's library. Rarely, he has found, does it ever contain a book in biblical studies or theology that was not a required text in seminary. Such libraries, however, do contain an enormous amount of theological "how to" and self-help books.

Farley's criticisms of theological education parallel the questions of coherence that many educators raise about liberal arts education, for both seem to have lost wisdom as their goal. Where does the solution lie? For Farley, it may lie in recovering the Christian counterpart of the ancient Greek notion of *paideia*, an education in excellence of character and an agreement through out the church on intellectual and moral ideals. A similar recovery in the liberal arts would be the retrieval of a sense of the unity of knowledge and its attendant wisdom. Yet there may be more than a parallel here, there may also be a link. A sense of the unity of human knowing may be important for a lively sense of the Creator, while a sense of the Creator may be essential for believing in an ultimate unity of knowledge and activity.

This is not a new idea. Such a connection provides the basis of much of the history of education in the West. Plato's analogy of the cave in the *Republic*, whereby a soul is liberated from the bonds of sense and led to a vision of the Good—Plato's equivalent to God—is quickly followed by a curriculum designed to be useful for attaining that vision. In it a student mounts step by step towards a knowledge of the wisdom that rules the universe and each step is determined by the goal. Although Plato's curriculum did not become the curriculum of the classical liberal arts, his idea that education should lead to this sort of knowledge was not dropped. Throughout the Roman period it was assumed that "philosophy"—divine wisdom—is the goal of learning the *trivium* and *quadrivium* of the liberal arts, although as with us, both the goal and teaching of the curriculum in its entirety tended to receive little more than lip service.[11]

In many ways Christianity simply adopted the classical system of education, although the goal of philosophy became the goal of "Christian philosophy," a term that did not become "theology" until the medieval period. Numerous patristic writers, including Clement of Alexandria, Gregory of Nyssa and Augustine all saw this Christian philosophy as the goal of education. Soon after his conversion Augustine undertook to write a series of books on the liberal arts intended to show how their ordering was essential in the soul's coming to a knowledge of God. Although he only wrote two books before abandoning the project, Augustine's truly great work on Christian education, *On Christian Teaching*, is the later completion of one part of the project.

This Platonic-Augustinian way of relating the liberal arts and theology, however, did not simply confine the arts to the role of stepping-stones. Instead, each of the arts was considered important in itself because it included implicit theological knowledge, which is the key to leading the soul towards explicit theological knowledge. The liberal arts were not "skills" in the sense we understand the term, but microcosms of theology. Theology was not only the goal, but the very thing that made sense of human knowledge and art and gave them their unity and purpose. To participate in the arts at all was to have at least implicit knowledge of theology.

Perhaps the best illustration of this scheme can be taken from St. Bonaventure in the thirteenth century. In a small treatise titled, "The Reduction of the Arts to Theology," he undertook to show how all human knowledge ultimately flows from God. He included in that knowledge not only the liberal arts (to which the natural sciences belonged) but also the mechanical arts of the workaday world such as carpentry and farming. Bonaventure's confidence that all the arts could be traced to one source came from a passage in the Epistle of James: "Every good gift is from the Father of lights in whom there is no change." Reasoning that the arts were good gifts, Bonaventure then proceeded to show how the arts offer a threefold analogy of God's own action. First he links the productions of works of art to the incarnation of Christ; in each case there is an idea or interior "word" made visible. The second analogy links the effect of each of these arts and the pattern of human life intended by God for the artisan means his work to be beautiful, useful and enduring; God intends this for our lives. A third analogy links the delight we take in the arts with the union of the soul to God, which is the greatest delight of all. Because there are these analogies, he reasoned, each art shows the mark of its origin and thus "all branches of knowledge have their origin in the one light." All our knowledge, no matter how diverse, is from one source. Furthermore all our knowledge, if we understand it correctly, leads back to that source.

The Platonic-Augustinian view was not the only one, of course. Yet even Thomas Aquinas, who did not try to reduce all knowledge to different forms of theological knowledge, thought that the arts should be "ordered to theology" as their capstone. Aquinas understood knowledge to be structured as a "hierarchy of discourses;" careful teaching directs students upwards through the hierarchy to the limits of human knowledge in metaphysics. Theology—the knowledge gained from studying revelation—completes and fulfills our knowledge. In many Catholic liberal arts colleges today, such ordering is still an explicit criterion in curricular decisions.

That is not the case, however, in most liberal arts colleges. Few school catalogues proclaim a reduction or ordering of the arts to theology. Yet there are vestiges. A hundred years ago the mandatory course for all seniors in natural theology, or "evidences of Christianity," was one such vestige; the contemporary claim to educate "the whole person" is another, particularly if the claim involves some sense of wisdom as well as skill. Yet as the flurry of curriculum changes continues in American higher education, it seems that this is precisely what is not taking place. Why?

One reason is simply that modern knowledge does not show much evidence of the unity of things. Rightly or wrongly, it is the only knowledge we have. It would be incredibly naive to try to assume a world view such as Bonaventure possessed. He may give us correctives and signposts for trying to conceive of a unified view, but he cannot give us that unity itself. And at present nobody else seems to be able to do so. There is no super theory or science that has put it all together.

As a modern problem, it is perhaps insoluble. But there is another question bearing on the unity of knowledge that can concern us, and it is this. How, in all their diversity, do the knowledge and the texts of a particular culture belong together? In asking this question, we are asking not for a theoretical unity, but a unity that will be reflected in the thought and action of a culture's heirs. We are asking how people can make diverse knowledge cohere in their lives; how they can focus ideas into a single ray of wisdom.

I do not think this question is asked very often, though; much of contemporary education may even be working away from such a goal. By teaching knowledge as a series of discrete fields we rarely attempt any sort of wholistic approach. Students are offered electives and required to pick "majors" that will train them as experts in one area; rarely at the end of their education will they be able to converse with people who have a different speciality. With no means of even rudimentary conversation with other interests and specialities, students will make little attempt to wrestle with the problem. Thus not only have we and our students lost the vision of unified knowledge, we have lost the desire to find it.

Even the broad-based curriculum, which requires or encourages exposure to numerous fields in order to combat this over-specialization, is no more than a weak practical antidote. The lesson that these fields simply do not connect is quickly learned. Even the attempted remedy in many schools of requiring interdisciplinary courses rarely helps much. The intention is excellent. Yet where each department sails under the flag of a special method and discipline, the interdisciplinary course merely advertises the problem that these fields do not relate well. Since the course itself generally lacks a discipline—which is all important to the minds of almost everyone concerned—it is considered trivial.

One good remedy, of course, would be to insist that all courses be taught with an eye to other forms of knowledge, asking what their connections might be to the present object of study. Yet the outlook for this approach is hardly sanguine. It is rare that humanities professors speak of mathematics or physics in their courses, still rarer that biology professors either mention or know in any detail the history of their own field. This is not surprising since few teachers have been educated this way themselves.

Another reason for this loss of a unified vision may lie in the reduced status of theology in the curriculum. In order to make this problem clear, let us imagine the ideal relationship between philosophy, the quest for understanding and wisdom, and theology, the quest for the knowledge of God. The ideal picture, which is readily recognizable from the ancient and medieval church, involves a relation between philosophy and theology in which philosophy is seen as a kind of prologue to theology. Philosophy suggests to the mind questions about "God and the soul" to which the mind can only find satisfactory answers in the truths of Christianity. Justin Martyr, Augustine and numerous others tell us how philosophy has done just this for them. In this ideal relationship philosophy does not merely lead one up to theology, to the door of revelation, it also leads back to the world from revelation. It is philosophy that is the tool that enables theology to become a discipline; with the addition of philosophy, theology involves not only vision, but also reason. It is now something that can be used to spread the knowledge of God.

This picture is entrancing and it is ancient. It is even, I suspect, still widely held. It is a philosopher's picture of how we approach ultimate reality. But there is a problem. The problem does not lie with the picture as an ideal, but with the fact that we have no means to reach the ideal. Students who would approach theology in this way are in no position to so. Let us see some reasons why.

In the first place, philosophy as currently practiced and taught also suffers from compartmentalization. It is rarely about a whole vision and an ultimate purpose. Particularly in Anglo-American philosophy, it has tended to concentrate on discrete problems, many of which are technical and mainly of interest to other philosophers. After Wittgenstein, for example, philosophy saw a rash of "maps" and "grammars" of various words and concepts. This has been very important, and has even borne fruit in theological disciplines. Nevertheless it is hardly the sort of thing that leaves students in a tense wonderment that can only be aided by revelation. The courses in "natural theology" of the last century, if taught today, would not have any knowledge of which they would be the capstone; virtually nothing taught in the curriculum today would lead to such a topic of learning.

In the one area of the curriculum where we hope students will gain some sense of a broad unifying vision, a wisdom that allows them to participate in the larger body, there we meet fragmentation again. Philosophy rarely leads us to the door of theology very often. If and when students arrive at it by other means, they are rarely articulate about the questions that need to be raised about it. Because they cannot think very well in terms of the whole, it becomes rather easy to privatize faith—instead of seeing how it embraces and directs our whole life, including our understanding. It is easy to fence the knowledge of God off from the knowledge we might have about God's creation.

Another factor is the loss of theology itself as a subject taught in most mainline Protestant colleges, or just about anywhere else besides seminaries. "Religion" is taught in colleges; sometimes it is even required. But "religious studies" is not the same thing as theology. Unlike theology, religious studies presupposes neither a starting point of faith nor a culminating vision. Instead it concerns itself with *what* religious people think. It does not encourage them to do this religious thinking well. Therefore religious studies does not even pretend to create new thought about God, or to give thought about God wider and more comprehensive meaning, although it does provide vital information about religion. And even when religion is taught meaning fully, its larger goal of unifying the life and thought of the believer is generally ignored.

Hence the very notion of the whole person disintegrates when wholeness appears to be either a false or an unattainable ideal. Without this sense of wholeness, there can be no meaning to *paideia*, no thought for the unity of a culture nor wise participation in it. There is only room for an endless number of specialists.

One obvious remedy to the present situation would be to teach philosophy and theology differently. It might even be desirable to require a freshman course that introduced students to liberal arts education, where their minds might be disabused of the notion that they were about to receive a purely vocational education. They would have to see that the education on which they were about to embark is designed to help them participate meaningfully in something larger. If this could be done, then these freshmen might be able to make more of the course of study on which they are about to embark. Similarly, a course for seniors might be added to the curriculum, one where they could focus the rays of their acquired knowledge by setting it in an ultimate context.

Such solutions, however, will be futile in the absence of a larger sense of the unity of the whole curriculum. If we are to move students to full participation in the culture or the divine body, we might borrow from Bonaventure and attempt to reimagine how each part of the curriculum both participates in and is validated by the larger whole. Just as the study of religion needs the broader context of lived activity, so too any school that aims at educating the whole person ought to provide broader ongoing intellectual activity than one finds in schools that aim at merely preparing students for a profession. What I am suggesting is a sort of "theology of curriculum," to use a phrase that is sufficiently modern in its awkwardness. By it I mean a sense of wholeness and ultimacy to the search for wisdom that inspires and pervades the entire curriculum.

What I mean by this "pervasive" theology is best illustrated by looking at some specific liberal arts curricula. On one end of the spectrum is the socalled "smorgasbord" approach, where there are few if any specific requirements, as well as a great deal of encouragement to pursue courses in many different fields. This type is best exemplified by Brown University, which not only originated it, but has continually worked to improve it. Second, there is the "core curriculum" approach, in which a certain number of courses within specific areas of the sciences and humanities are required, with the remainder distributed between the student's major field and free electives. This type is the most common in liberal arts colleges across the country. Third, there is a form exemplified by many Catholic liberal arts colleges; it resembles the second type, but, following Aquinas, it deliberately places theology at the summit of knowledge. All other courses are thought to lead to theology. Finally, at the other end of the spectrum is the Great Books approach, exemplified by St. John's College, in which there are no electives and where primary works are read almost exclusively.

The last two types best show a "theology of curriculum." Both are shaped by a very explicit philosophy of education and the student is always very much aware of it. Both have some more or less defined vision of wisdom as the true end of education. Both assume that wisdom can be found through an intensive dialogue with the most important texts of the culture, the very texts that have been largely responsible for creating and sustaining the culture. Both seek a wisdom that involves quality of thought and life; such wisdom is not simply the result of a mere knack, but the intelligent participation in and use of the larger community. Neither form of education is a mere preparation for a profession, although they are not irrelevant to a career, either.

At the same time, their differences are striking. Whereas the Thomistic approach makes revealed theology a privileged art, and thus aims consciously at Christian theological knowledge, the Great Books curriculum, at least at St. John's, has a different task. It is to analyze and discuss each text on its own terms, theological or not. Nietzche, for example, is to be discussed with the same seriousness as the Gospel of St. John. Whether Nietzche or St. John will continue to reward such seriousness is not decided ahead of time for the student, even though a particular seminar might reach a consensus on one or the other. Thus it is not unusual for the Bible and the Church Fathers to come in for a thrashing in the seminar; it is also not unusual for the participating students to arrive at an even deeper appreciation.

Some of the differences between the two approaches were highlighted in a threeday discussion that took place some years ago at St. John's in Santa Fe under the auspices of the National Endowment for the Humanities. On the second day of the discussion a heated dispute arose between the representatives of St. John's and Thomas Aquinas College in Santa Paula, California. The latter follows a Great Books curriculum, but Christian theology is its acknowledged core and other fields are ordered around it. In the dispute the Aquinas representative maintained that theology is a privileged art, which defines the relationships of all the others; St. John's maintained that this illegitimately subordinated one field to another and introduced majors into the liberal arts. The St. John's people took an "agnostic view;" they refused to assume any field as normative.

In the course of the discussion, however, some interesting points of agreeement surfaced about the unity of knowledge. If St. John's refused to assign the unifying factor of the curriculum to a specific field, nevertheless they saw the unity of knowledge as a concern that lay at the very heart of their education. One person summed up the discussion by noting that, indeed, there were deep differences, but also common ground in their mutual belief that the whole of knowledge is an integral part of the liberal arts.

That common ground is also an overriding concern for a wisdom that seeks the self-transcendence of the student. The student learns to view the goal of knowledge as more than the sum of its parts, attainable through a deeper rootedness within the culture. Yet while Aquinas attempted to realize these goals through Christian theology, St. John's did not. Even there, the differences were not absolute. Both addressed a common theological concern, the student's transcendence of a limited self. Aquinas' view of this self-transcendence was simply guided by confessional standards. At St. John's, however, explicit Christian theology is not ruled out, despite the school's pedagogical agnosticism. For it may very well turn out that a student's transcendence of self is best realized through Christian theology. Simply including readings of important works of Christian theology impresses upon students that theology is an important and live option to consider. Although it is not a college with church ties, St. John's may very well succeed in making theology a discipline more essential to its curriculum than it is in many church-related schools that isolate it and set it off as merely another department. In isolation, theology ceases to be considered a means to wisdom.

It is interesting to note, by the way, that a significant percentage of St. John's graduates do go on to careers in the Christian ministry and in theology. It has probably a higher percentage of such graduates than virtually any Presbyterian college.

This concern for the unity of knowledge evidenced by this brief debate is an important signal to the liberal arts. It shows that a concern for wisdom is the goal of liberal education. One college, for obvious and good reasons, has determined that wisdom to be accessible through Christian theology proper; the other, without rejecting this as a possibility, pays important attention to wisdom in other ways. Yet it is a common passion for wisdom that orders the arts at both schools—as it ordered them originally for the Greeks. For this reason their form of education, even if it differs outwardly from the ancient Greeks, is truly *paideia*.

The "pervasive" theology I have noted is easily seen in a "Great Books" education; a sense of ultimacy affects each course within the curriculum. Not only does it influence decisions about what courses will be offered, but just as important, how both students and teachers view knowledge. Far from being ideology—students take away some very independent views from a Great Books education—this sense of ultimacy gives an all-important context for knowledge. By seeking a cohering ultimacy to life, this education also challenges students to fuse the many aspects of what they have learned. Both they and the school are convinced that knowledge ultimately contributes to the excellence of inner being and to the realization of moral and intellectual ideals.

What about the two other forms of liberal education? Probably no one form of liberal education need to be considered purer than another. Paradoxically, often the "smorgasbord" curriculum may approach the non-elective Great Books curriculum in spirit best, even though its method seems to be a polar opposite. Such an approach can combat a tendency to specialize studies too early, encouraging students to seek a vision of unity. In one sense such a vision is its very purpose; given sufficient institutional and faculty encouragement, this approach can be extremely effective in opening students to a larger vision of the whole. It may even open up theological thinking as a possibility, although students also have the means of avoiding it completely. One simply has to rely on a student's own sense of curiosity and her need for an integrating vision. Similarly, any form of education can be helpful if it offers sufficient opportunity and encouragement to do this.

Yet can we assume that if students achieve this goal—wisdom—it does not matter how they get there? The liberal arts do not invariably produce a love of wisdom, a sense of coherence and meaning, and an ability to participate in a culture of shared values. The possibility of these goals being achieved rises only when the need to find coherence is not undermined by the curriculum. One of the points of education is to make things clearer to students; if this vision of the unity of knowledge is obscured, then students will discover it only by accident. Because so many schools divide themselves into departments and these departments decide curricular affairs, there is a tendency to regard each field as the provenance of an isolated expertise. It is amazing how many professors will extol the virtues of the liberal arts, but who then object whenever the demands of the curriculum threaten to keep their majors from a lockstep approach to professional expertise. One finds this attitude frequently among those science professors who refuse to count the sciences among the liberal arts, although the sciences have always been an essential component. In such cases, the goal of the unity of knowledge is constantly being undermined.

The key to the development of the whole person through the liberal arts is empowering students to feel at home with what the human mind can know—and to accept what it cannot know. Ideally, a liberal arts education initiates a quest to know that will continue throughout the rest of one's life. It is not simply the acquiring of skills, although they are certainly required as tools of understanding. But in order to feel at home with knowledge human beings need to know that knowledge itself can cohere, that it ought to be integrated. We no longer possess any believable grand metaphysical schemes which promise to unite all knowledge into a single system, so we cannot take that coherence on authority. Yet we do possess through the greatest books of our culture a witness to the importance of the effort to find coherence. In many cases these books still have what count as knowledge; what is more important, though, is that they possess wisdom—even where they are factually wrong. This is why it is a crime to dismiss them to simply as precursors of more "advanced" or specialized modern knowledge or as a storehouse of "great opinions." They do not belong to any particular field; they belong together to teach us to make the effort of integrating knowledge. They teach us wisdom because that is what they are about.

Because we have lost a sense of the unity of those texts that have shaped our culture, we have also lost a way to appreciate a common good or sense within society as a whole, to say nothing of an important unifying factor in individual experience. The crucial significance of this loss is something that needs to be taken seriously in the present wave of curricular reform; such reforms rarely look for any principle of wisdom that can unite the disparate parts. If an individual professor searches for such a principle, too often she goes no farther than the limits of her own discipline. As disciplines clash, as departments worry about how reform is going to affect their numbers of students and their influence within the institution as a whole, curriculum reform tends to degenerate into a battle over turf. So the actual reform may involve no more than cosmetic changes; even when the appearance of change is great, the fundamental mindset has not been changed at all.

A far better approach to curriculum reform would first clarify what sort of person the school expects to graduate and by what standards he should be considered wise. How far does he go beyond mere technical knack, and what sorts of principles does he embody in his thought and action? A whole person, one who is at home with human knowledge, ought to be the goal. Before embarking on reform, it may be wise to undertake a period of study and reflection on what a wise person actually is. In itself, such a study may either show a unity to the curriculum that was hidden before, to be revealed only by teaching, or produce a sense of unity and purpose that had been lacking before. Such a study may even have the salutary effect on faculties and administrations that the liberal arts is meant to have on students.

The knowledge of what makes a wise person is sufficiently ambiguous to allow numerous interpretations. But to some degree it ought to do so, since the character and possibilities of faculties and student bodies vary so greatly. What one needs to be wise in Cambridge, Massachusetts does not overlap entirely with what one needs in a largely rural area in the Midwest. Nevertheless, the Cantabrigian and the Decaturite, if they are wise, ought to be able to converse meaningfully about human purpose and strive within their culture for some overriding common good. Their ability to do so will largely depend upon whether their education has given them a sufficiently deep well of common tradition at which to drink and their ability to transcend narrow personal issues in order to imagine a larger whole.

This much needs to be said of any liberal arts education. How it is to be instituted remains in the hands of those responsible for curricular reform. The task within the church-related colleges, however, is less ambiguous. Their standards of wisdom are not governed by a sort of "natural theological wisdom," but by revealed theology. Even if Christian theology is not deliberately used as the prime means to wisdom, it at least ought not to be placed in the position of seeming irrelevant to that wisdom. Even if the church colleges do not explicitly aim at theological wisdom, what they do aim at ought to be useful as a means of finding the wisdom that is the knowledge of God. This, above all, will constitute the value of any college to the church, for the recovery of the liberal arts tradition of aiming towards a unity of knowledge and its accompanying wisdom is an important step towards recovering what Farley calls *theologia*. For Christians the wisdom that accompanies the wisdom of knowledge, if it is not *theologia* itself, is the condition for any intellectual apprehension of it—unless, of course, one happens to believe that Athens has nothing to do with Jerusalem.

Chapter Five

Making A Faith

As a whole, student reaction to any given college course is invariably mixed, ranging from utter boredom and disinterest to the feeling that the course has changed their lives. Positive reactions usually depend upon the course having awakened and fulfilled a real need. I have, for example, often found that students who have gotten the most out of religion courses are those who already actively religious. For these students the knowledge they gain is important because it allows them to deepen a faith which is already important to them. The reaction of these students has always struck me because it confirms a remark once made by a friend of mine about American religion. He observed that far too much of American religion is based on a revival tent model, with preachers trying constantly to convert their hearers. Yet too often that is preaching to the converted. What Christians want to hear and what they need to hear is not what to believe, but *how* to believe. They need to know how to get from step A to step B of the spiritual life and yet all they hear are pleas to get to step A when they have been there all the time.

Hugh Kerr, the longtime editor of *Theology Today*, once suggested that among the most pertinent of contemporary religious issues is, "Young people today want to know how to make a faith." However, they are not often being given this knowledge. Kerr thinks that the fault for this situation is various. On the one hand, it is sometimes the fault of profes-

sional academic theology. The great theological names of our
century—Barth, Brunner, Niebuhr—have consistently ignored the area of personal religious experience. They have
given us a theology of light, but not a theology of life. They
have told us what life in God should be but they have not told
us how to get there—nor even if it is possible to get there,
given who we are. Take as an example the seminary professor who wrote an article on the political implications of the
Trinity. After it was published one of his graduate students
slyly pointed out that it seemed the man fully expected middle-class people to take to the streets and start a revolution in
the name of the triune God. The Trinity indeed may have implications for our life together, but I doubt that few political
revolutions have recently arisen out of a rigorous analysis of
inter-trinitarian relation, nor are they likely to.

The fault, however, does not lie entirely with academic
theology but with the expectations of believers, who have little sense of the importance of belonging to a larger body. Kerr
may be overly optimistic when he says that college students
want to know how to make a faith. Many, I think, want nothing of the kind. Among those who are interested at all, many
want to be handed a faith just as they want to be handed
knowledge to carry out a profession. This does not mean they
are like spoiled children who believe that the world owes
them a living. Rather, they are unsure of themselves and of
the world they live in; they want certainty, for these do not
seem appropriate times to risk experiment. Yet unfortunately
no one can give them that certainty, for the world has never
been certain. Whatever certainty faith may bring can only be
obtained by experiment and experience.

One needs to "make" a faith; it cannot simply be acquired
and left untended. Faith is not simply obstinate intellectual
belief; it is a way of life that requires both knowledge *and*
practice. It requires practice as Pascal understood it. In a
well-known passage from his *Pensees* he argues to a gambler
that it is a much better wager to believe and possibly gain

everything than not to believe and lose all. Even though the gambler is convinced, he still cannot bring himself to believe. The cure, Pascal says, is not additional proofs, it is "to learn of those who have been bound like you, and who now stake all their possessions ...Follow the way by which they began; by acting as if they believed, taking the holy water, having masses said, etc."[12]

Faith also requires knowledge, though. Without knowledge, it is mere superstition and merely "making up" a faith, as many people have mistakenly assumed Pascal to have suggested. Yet despite our fear of acting hypocritically many people do end up adopting some kind of faith and going through its motions without ever growing in that faith. The French philosopher Alain under stood the phenomenon well and told a story to illustrate it. It is the story of Balaoo, a monkey who was taught to speak and dress like a man. Now this monkey used to go to the zoo of the *Jardin des Plantes* at night to pick up his brother Gabriel, and after dressing him properly, would take him around to the cabarets. Unfortunately Gabriel had the habit of throwing himself on anything he wanted, such as a lady's hat decorated with artificial flowers, which, needless to say, caused a commotion. Finally Balaoo taught Gabriel the following lesson: "When humans want to eat something, they don't just take it; they have to show their intentions by putting down some money." Alain goes on to observe that children think of money this way. For them, the exchange of money is simply ritual behaviour that has to be gone through in order to get the object of their desire. They do not see that it is *labor* that gets what we want—albeit through the intermediary of money. Too often in faith we behave like such children, thinking that our prayers, hymns and sighings of the spirit are ritual behaviours of the human world that inexplicably, and for frivolous reasons, have to go between what we want and what we get. We lack knowledge of what we are doing. Just as adults are differentiated from children by understanding labor, so too are spiritual adults distinguished from spiritual children by knowing the labor of faith.

Students need to know the content of faith in order to get beyond superstition. They need to know, for example, that faith is not obstinate intellectual belief, the profoundly satisfying intellectual depth at which religion can be thought. The sense that religion is important is often awakened in students just by their having to pay close attention to religious texts, when they suddenly discover that there is more there than they had ever learned in Sunday School. Yet even for students who have gotten this far, there is more to learn. A high percentage of students who are spiritually awake, for example, still have little sense of the importance of the communities in which they live their lives. Many of these students see faith strictly as a personal quest—an individual matter. Yet as one bright young woman I knew soon realized, she had nobody to talk to about what was most important to her; she had, in fact, dedicated herself to an isolated pilgrimage. Consequently the search for faith which was truly important to her became in her life only a passing "phase."

The need for students to know how to make a faith sets an important task for the Christian liberal arts tradition. Even though that tradition shares much common ground with secular forms of education, it has certain specific questions, unique to itself, which it must address. One question it needs to address is what the specific ends of Christianity are and how one can think about them properly—and distinguish them from other ends. The means that exist to attain those ends are important, too. These questions must be addressed at a depth beyond mere theory. Even if Christian liberal arts schools are primarily concerned with intellectual education and cannot be expected to compel faith, nevertheless they need to make students aware of what the life of faith really is.

The importance of this knowledge and how it is related to the actual practice of faith is well illustrated by the biblical example of Thomas the doubter. The story of doubting Thomas is one we all learn early on in Sunday school, even though we would not usually say that it is a story of one of the great heroes of the faith. In fact the usual moral drawn from the Thomas story is that we should *not* be like Thomas; his main function is to serve as a bad example.

But why do we look down on Thomas this way? In asking to see and touch Jesus before he would believe that Jesus was risen from the dead, Thomas was really asking for no more than any of the other disciples, all of whom had seen Jesus in one of his previous appearances. Thomas alone was absent, and yet he seems to be held in low regard because he asks for proof. Proof, even if it is possible in a matter of faith, appears to be part of a never-ending process. Once we begin, we will never come to faith, since there is always one more bit of evidence that we need before we can conclude our investigations. There are simply some things for which we cannot have proof, so this criticism of Thomas runs, and if we are to take advantage of them we must take them on faith—whatever that means.

Yet when I reflect upon these ideas, I think that this is not what the story of Thomas is about. When we look carefully at the story we do not find Thomas asking for proof that Jesus is God; we do not even see him asking for proof that Jesus is Jesus. An ancient tradition claimed that John the Evangelist calls Thomas "the twin" because he was Jesus' twin, or resembled him closely. If anything like this is true, then it is obvious that one glance at Jesus would have been sufficient to convince Thomas of the Lord's identity.

What then was Thomas asking for? What was the evidence he required? It was only one thing—that he be allowed to put his fingers in the nail holes of Christ's hand. Now, we think that this request just goes to show what kind of person Thomas was, one who had to touch and feel before he will accept anything as true. He seems the ancient prototype of the modern hardline empiricist.

Yet seen another way, what Thomas asks for should really convince us of the fact that he was a man of deep faith. Perhaps alone of all the disciples, Thomas had actually listened to all that Jesus had said to them and taught them before his crucifixion. Thomas had spent enough time with Jesus to know that there is only one way, one form of evidence, by which we can recognize the risen Lord: he bears the marks of the crucifixion. The risen Christ is Lord only because he is the crucified Christ. The book of *Revelation* even goes so far as to point out that Christ bears these marks even in his eternal glory. In this sense Thomas is no doubter at all; the proof he asks for is the proof that Christ himself taught him to request. Far from a doubter, Thomas is an excellent student. In this sense he is also an excellent example of how Christians ought to learn.

The point of the Thomas example may be seen in comparison to the answer John Calvin once gave to the question of why the Apostles' Creed only contains a few facts of Christ's life, such as his birth, suffering, death and resurrection. Why, Calvin was asked, is there no mention of Christ's teaching, which after all occupies such a large place in all the gospels? He replied that such things as we do recite in the creed are all that is needed for salvation. It is not because Jesus taught the multitudes that we are reconciled to God; it is because he died.

Calvin's answer is correct in relation to the faith we hold; however, this does not mean Jesus' teaching is irrelevant to our coming to hold that faith. If we ignore the teaching, we may also miss the facts of salvation. We need that teaching to distinguish true from false. We need that teaching to know good from evil and to know the difference between true life and all the imitations with which we are constantly faced. Thomas listened to that teaching and he recognized the difference between truth and falsehood. It was *only* through listening to that teaching that he recognized Christ among all the false messiahs who competed for his allegiance and affection. Because of this teaching which instructed his mind, Thomas knew the ends of his heart. And when he saw the satisfaction of those ends of his heart standing in front of him, he cried out "My Lord and my God."

The example of Thomas shows us the need for teaching even in the realm of faith. But it also illustrates at a deeper level the point that I have tried to make already; facts are important chiefly within the larger context of value. It was because Thomas valued Jesus' sacrificial death that he asked to be shown the facts—in this case, the nailmarks. No other fact would have convinced him. It was because Thomas valued a certain way of living, which he in time would be expected to emulate, that he asked for certain facts. It was because of what he understood a saviour really to be be that he found certain facts about him important.

There are, however, two particular problems that this observation raises for the teaching of religion in an academic setting if it is to contribute to shaping the whole person. First of all, it cannot content itself simply with presenting the "facts" of Christianity, as so in many religion courses do. Students must know what Christians believe, the history of Christianity and the biblical story, but that is not enough. Rather, it is essential that the ultimate meaning of these facts be made as evident as possible so that they might be valued. This is a point that might be made of any other subject. But Christian higher education also faces a second problem, for knowledge as it is commonly understood today does not include much room for the valuing of religion.

The distinction we make between facts and values is not simply an accidental and arbitrary bit of cultural prejudice. Instead, it lies very deep in the western thinking of the last three hundred years and is found also at the base of modern scientific thinking, which we have elevated to a nearly unassailable position. The reason the distinction is so important is, in short, because it guarantees the formulaic truth of science. Facts by definition are independent of the observer—

regardless of her state of mind or her personal background and character. Once the fact is stated it simply is, in all of its eternal and unchangeable splendor. Of course we can be wrong about the facts we hold, but even the notion of being wrong is here understood in comparison to a strict standard of factuality. Facts are either plain to everybody, or they can be rigorously demonstrated. Values, however, are different since they can only be understood by persons of character. We can rigorously demonstrate the accuracy of the mathematical laws of gravitation to anybody; how, though, do you demonstrate to an egotist the value of self-sacrifice for the benefit of others? If he is insensitive to other people, there is no place we could even begin such a demonstration. Nail marks would not prove a thing to him. Values are thus thought to be "subjective," lacking the rigor and universality of facts.

Recent work in the philosophy of science, such as that of Putnam, has argued, often very convincingly, against the "myth of the neutral observer." No fact is independent of thinking minds and their history of lived values. Even so, such work has done little to dispel the notion outside the the academy. It simply seems too basic to us, although it is actually relatively new within western culture. The notion is not easy to dispel, either, particularly in a culture that has a strong technical education but little firsthand acquaintance with what the best minds of the western tradition actually thought prior to the Enlightenment. Gadamer has argued forcefully that even humanistic disciplines such as history, where one would expect to find some alternative way of thinking, have deliberately modelled themselves on the methods used in the physical sciences. These disciplines, perhaps more than science itself, are responsible for hardening the myth into a "fact," since they refuse to challenge it.

In much of contemporary Western thought, therefore, there is very little of a humanistic understanding of human life and values, only a scientific one. The problem this creates in trying to teach the meaning of religion is enormous. On the one hand, its meaning is usually heard and evaluated by students in inadequate scientistic terms. The meaning of creation is completely opaque to students who can only think of creation as an argument between Darwin and the Bible. Teachers are often more sophisticated, but have difficulty getting much beyond the level of asking whether Thomas *could* have put his fingers in the holes. To go further is to transgress the limits of the empirical methodology in which they were trained—it would exceed the facts they hope to get their colleagues to accept. That is hardly the spirit in which Thomas sought for the evidence of Jesus' identity.

There is a vicious circle here. At the same time that students need to make a faith, they are hardly in a position to understand when they are actually taught how to do so. Even when the teacher is good, they misunderstand what they hear him saying. Misunderstanding is then piled upon misunderstanding by a method of teaching that tries to get students to be rational by paying strict attention to the facts.

There thus arises a particularly nasty problem. It might be described as a gross confusion between the ends of the heart, which teach us to recognize the valuable, and the means of the mind, which teach us how to achieve it. The confusion reigns in every realm of our lives; we try to be toughminded and intellectual, and so miss the love that surrounds us, or we try to be open and affectionate and end up being only sentimental and sloppy. In intellectual life this confusion is witnessed to by scientism, the belief that apart from the scientific no forms of knowledge exist, that there is nothing to know beyond this world, or at least nothing we can know. Such a belief denies that there is any legitimate end for the heart at all. Instead, the means of the mind, which are meant to show us what is worth loving, have become an end in themselves. But the confusion also reigns in religion and ethics whenever we believe that what the heart loves overrides the considerations of hard thought. Too often in faith what is true and false is only true or false because we want it to be that way, because somehow, it is said, we believe it in our hearts.

Science is not alone to blame for this confusion of mind and heart. Practicing scientists make modest enough claims. The confusion arises in good part because people do not know how to think religiously and science is used to fill the void. Unfortunately, there has been little attempt at correction— particularly within state universities, which fear they may be overstepping the constitutional boundaries of church and state. One case introduced a few years ago involved the granddaughter of the well-known atheist, Madalyn Murray O'Hair. She brought suit against the University of Texas, which had introduced a course in Biblical Literature into the curriculum, although such courses were purely elective. Ms. O'Hair claimed in her suit that such courses serve no secular purpose. What is most distressing about the case is its assumption that such courses can serve no intellectual purpose and so can easily be omitted from the curriculum without shortchanging the students. It also assumes that there is only one way of thinking, and that is by empirical and scientific means.

Unfortunately, as courses of study that would teach us to recognize something of value beyond the empirical are driven from the university, the harder it becomes for us to recognize any thing beyond what we can touch and feel. When we reach the point that we cannot recognize anything but our own five senses, our minds have totally replaced our hearts. Strangely enough, such an outcome will reduce most other courses to the pragmatic—and hence to the static and boring—since they no longer seem to be serving any higher purpose.

The confusion of heart and mind is actually a danger both to science and to religion. As we become incapable of thinking religiously, we also fail to see the limits of science. We can no longer respect its real power, nor understand what a proper investigation of the physical world really is.

Some years ago Carl Sagan, the Cornell astronomer presented a program on public television entitled "Cosmos." It was intended to present both a history of cosmological thinking and a contemporary understanding of it. The show was glossy and very well received; however, it had two particularly odious features. The first was Sagan's obvious disdain for religion and his misunderstanding of the role religion has played in scientific thinking. According to him, religion's role has been only a negative one in scientific research; it has attempted to thwart research at every turn. Not only did the church mercilessly persecute Galileo, its "superstitious" dogmas in every age have been thoroughly hostile to the quest for truth. Yet Sagan refused to acknowledge that almost all of his heroes of science, from the Greeks to Einstein, were people of deep religious conviction. These convictions were what motivated them to undertake their researches in the first place.

Copernicus, for example, did not place the sun at the center of our planetary system because he could prove it—he couldn't —but because, he argued, it is the heavenly body most like God and so belongs at the center. Moreover, his (erroneous) belief that the planets moved around the sun in regular circles was justified by his assumption that it was more perfect and regular than any other way, and God always does things in the best way possible. When Kepler undertook to correct Copernicus, he did so with the explicit belief that he would discover the mystical harmony of the solar system, the one God had ordained. Religious conviction led these men to undertake their researches in the first place; their belief in a purposeful creator of the heavens gave them the confidence and hope in finding design in the universe. If these scientists had believed, on the contrary, that there is no discernible purpose in the world around us, they would have found it perfectly pointless to look for it. And what difference would it have made, anyhow? It was Einstein who said in a well-known remark, "I refuse to believe that God plays dice with

the universe." Because of this belief he thought he could discover the universe's design Thus Sagan's presentation ignored a very real and important relationship that has
historically existed between science and religion.

The second obnoxious aspect of Sagan's presentation,
however, is a deeply ironical one. He placed himself in the
position of high priest mediating deep scientific truths to the
laity, although many of these so-called truths (such as his
speculations on extra-terrestial life and the straight line
development of the universe) are speculative at best and most
probably only modern myths. Oddly enough, after trying hard
to get rid of religion, he finished by exalting science into a
new one. Unfortunately, it is this new religion that is most
likely to be superstitious and to prey upon the gullible. The
laity remains for the most part uneducated about scientific
matters and so unable to evaluate the meaning of Sagan's
pronouncements. Throughout its long development Christianity has at least has evolved rigorous ways to think
theologically, even if theological oddballs continually appear. In fact, it is precisely because of these oddballs that
Christianity has seen the need to do so. Yet I suspect many
people were deeply impressed by Sagan. Perhaps it is their
fault; perhaps it is the fault of the education which never
taught them how this all works.

The problem which a position like Sagan's raises for
education is twofold. On the one hand it is dangerous intellectually, since it is based on half truths. On the other hand it
also works against the development of the whole person by
encouraging gullible submission to authority, hardly a
desirable trait in those who ought to be contributing members
to the social whole. It does not allow for any sort of humility
in the holding of knowledge. In this regard, a great deal of
modern scholarship finds itself in a position similar to the one
Paul encountered in Corinth, which he writes about in I Corinthians. There, we may recall, Paul did not object so much to
the Corinthian's knowledge as the proud and bombastic at-

titudes it had led to. What Paul wanted for the Corinthians was a wisdom that is humble and serves others.

The knowledge which is often taught today, however, is rarely humble, nor does it require humble service from those who possess it. The knowledge we derived from splitting the atom unlocked one of the deepest secrets of the universe; what we did with that knowledge and continue to do is too well known to bear repeating. In philosophy we learn from Socrates that the unexamined life is not worth living, and that philosophy is the love of wisdom, yet philosophical journals are filled with articles by philosophers peppered with dismissals of their colleagues' work as "howlers," as "dark," "incoherent," and "incomprehensible." Among students we hear how much more rigorous one person's major is than another's; we see efforts by their teachers in faculty meetings to assert the same thing. One begins to appreciate the position taken by groups such as the Amish, who refuse to let their children be educated by the world. They may not know much that we would count as knowledge, but they wouldn't dream of touching a gun.

What, then, is the solution, and what role does the Christian liberal arts have to play in it? How, by giving an intellectual education, can it contribute to the making of a faith? There are, in fact, two areas, teaching and communal life, in which they are uniquely suited to play a substantial role. First, they are attempting to give a broad-based education which allows a greater degree of intellectual interaction between disciplines if the people involved are willing to interact. Second, they do attempt to maintain some sort of common life. Even more significant, such colleges can play this role because, unlike state universities, they do not have to be neutral, even though they must keep an open mind.

In good part, one solution to the problem depends upon scholarship, and there is currently a good deal of excellent scholarship on the relationship of science and religion. Professors should be aware of this and use it. But two further elements are even more basic. The first is a recognition of the deep, intimate connection between faith and knowledge. On the one hand, faith can barely exist without knowledge. As we have seen previously, Augustine understood this when he argued the need for knowledge to understand the depths of the Bible. We must, at the very least, have the natural and historical knowledge required to read the Bible with understanding. Without knowledge, faith is blind. As John Mackay, the late president of Princeton Seminary, put it, "There is a difference between being a fool for Christ and just being a damn fool." Knowledge, on the other hand, is also impossible without faith. It is impossible because we have to begin our thinking on the basis of something we take for granted, and because some kind of faith in some kind of value is essential to our knowing.

This recognition of the interdependence of faith and know ledge is, at its roots, the recognition of the larger context in which education must take place. However, it ought not to be taken as an attempt to fuse the two. Science must be taught as science; it can, nonetheless, be taught humanistically. Even though it retains its individual integrity and methods, scientific learning ought to be explicitly recognized as a form of education within a larger moral and personal context. Questions about the relation of science to this larger context need to be raised often in religion and philosophy courses, even in science courses. Scientific questions of religion also ought to be raised continually. If the two often seem to conflict, then that is all the better; they conflict even in the world outside the academy. Students desparately need the opportunity to think about the two together, and rarely outside the college will they ever have the chance. The Christian liberal arts college, since it aspires to be good education that is both intellectual and Christian, is one of the few places where both science and religion are discussed in all seriousness and integrity.

There is a second aspect to this solution, however, and it has to do with the way religion is taught. Too often religion is taught in terms of what it is "about," with both students and professors observing religion from the outside, looking "objectively" either at the words of the Bible or at the behavior of religious groups. This approach is important for giving "Religious Studies" a scientific character as a discipline. It also keeps the boundaries between academic teaching and catechesis clear. By itself, however, such an approach is misleading; it sees religion as another sort of philosophy or another way of explaining the world on a par with science and history. All of us who have ever taught religion courses can easily remember the numerous papers we have received on how religion is an explanation of the place of human beings in a universe not of their own making, or how the universe came to be. This is erroneous in two ways. First, it is historically inaccurate. Although the Book of Genesis begins with the creation, ancient Hebrew and later Christian belief does not. Rather it begins in the experience of grace, whether at the Red Sea or in Christ. It is only later that believers realize that in order for God to be all that is, that God must control the universe and be its creator. In fact, the ancient Hebrews first assumed the existence of gods other than Yahweh; they simply weren't allowed to worship them. It is only after they realized that in order for Yahweh to use the Assyrians as the "rod of his anger," God must also control the universe. It is at that point that the great thinking of the Old Testament on creation begins.

In the second place, it is inaccurate because whatever else religion is, it is not an explanation—at least in the way that science explains things. It is something else. Religion is first and foremost what Wittgenstein called a form of life, and it is prior to explanation. In Pascal's words, God is the living God of Abraham, Isaac and Jacob and not the god of the philosophers. What did Pascal mean by this? In religion, people are dealing with a real being who deals back with them. They are not simply talking about an abstraction that conveniently explains the origin of the world when they have

no other answer. Pascal correctly pointed out that religion is
something lived, just as our life with other human beings is
something lived. Religious life is a communion upon which
believers base their lives; those lives need to be considered
when judging religion. Think of the well-known passage from
the Letter to the Hebrews, where we are told, "Faith is the
assurance of things hoped for, the conviction of things not
seen"(11.1). This passage is often misunderstood to mean that
faith is absolutely inscrutable, a matter of complete credulity.
Because in religion we are concerned with unseen things, this
argument runs, we have to take them on blind faith. There is
no hard evidence.

But this is not what the passage means at all. Granted, God
is not seen or perceived by any of our senses. But that doesn't
mean we have no so-called hard evidence of God's existence.
We do according to Hebrews, and that evidence is our faith.
Faith does not mean simply believing, but the quality of a
person's life. This is a quality that comes from basic communion and trust in God. The evidence for God's existence
and goodness is not invisible, it is plain to be seen in the faithful lives of his children, as Hebrews goes on to illustrate by
citing the "clouds of witnesses" who by their lives have
demonstrated God's life.

The lived evidence of faith is important in two essential
ways. First, it is the evidence that is needed to make a faith;
as such, it is what needs to be taught. Yet it is also important
for reflecting upon religion itself, and so is basic to understanding what religion is. In order to understand what religion
is about, one cannot simply present the so-called facts of
religion without also looking at what power they might exercise over the one who looks at them. To teach religion this
way, one has to ask what the psalmist means when he declares
that the doing of the Law is a joyful thing, or what Thomas
means when he cries, "My Lord and my God." Then one is
asking for the evidence of faith and how it plays a role in
human lives. The answers do not compel belief; what they do

is to give faith some understanding. For those students for whom faith is a living option, it may indeed help make a life of faith.

Presenting the evidence of faith is crucial for making a faith and does not run counter to an open intellectual education. Instead it allows us to see, as we must, the range of human thought and experience. If one is truly considering the whole person numerous questions have to be raised, not all of which can be treated by scientific methods. For example, one is compelled ask questions of what constitutes evidence; religion shows us that it comes in different forms. One also needs to be concerned with the qualitative differences in our experience, and how we use experience of all different sorts to deepen our knowledge. Above all, one is also compelled to ask what unity, if any, there is to the differing forms of knowledge and to the human person which knows in so many different ways. In short, taking seriously the evidence of faith forces us to raise the questions that are basic to a liberal arts education.

Chapter Six

My Pews Used to be Filled With Kids Like You

Anybody who was a part of an American college campus in the 1960's and is still on campus now cannot have failed to have noticed the radical change in campus moods. Whereas the sixties were a time of social protest, activism, and interest in Camus, Sartre, Marcuse, albeit shallow interest at times, the eighties have seen a turn to more personal concerns and a view of college as the means to a career. Perhaps this change has been nowhere illustrated so well as in the "Doonesbury" cartoon strip that is now taped to the door of so many faculty members' offices. The strip portrays a professor finishing a lecture on Thomas Jefferson's view of basic rights and asking for comments. Met by silence, he mutters to himself, "Of course not, you're too busy getting it all down." He then launches into a tirade designed to draw the students out, declaring finally that Jefferson was the anti-Christ and that black is white. As the students still dutifully write this out in notes, he collapses and sighs, "Teaching is dead." His students say amongst themselves: "Boy, this course is getting really interesting!" "You said it. I didn't know half this stuff."

The change in campus mood has greatly affected campus ministry as well, as "Doonesbury" shows. In the early seventies during the Vietnam War era, Chaplain Scot Sloan decides to go out on a date for the first time since 1953. The lapse in his social life, he explains, is that he just couldn't take time

off from his civil rights activities and other excitements.
However, now that the administration is so unresponsive to
protests, Scot Sloan declares, "Richard Nixon is enough to
drive a man to heavy dating!" In the middle of the 1980's,
however, he introduces himself to the young Sal Doonesbury,
whose philosophy of life is to "party down," and Sal's room-
mate, who quips, "Oh-Oh, a man of the cloth. Better hide the
ashtrays! Just kidding." Chaplain Sloan then confides to his
exstudent Mike Doonesbury, "I gotta level with you Mike, it's
very disheartening. The campus today seems to be filled with
either budding nihilists like your brother or little droids who
just want to be fed the answers. My pews used to be filled
with kids like you who asked questions, who grappled with
their faith, who led examined lives." Unfortunately, Mike
cannot take time to talk because his carpool is waiting.

The change in campus mood has engendered confusion and
frustration in the ranks of chaplains and campus ministers,
just as it does in Scot Sloan. Many chaplains who were educated in the 1960s may very well have expected their ministries to be ones of leading great causes, of deep social
involvement, of grappling with the great issues of faith. But
things have changed. The issues chaplains are often interested
in are not at the top of the list of student priorities and they
have had often to labor in obscurity, their efforts ignored. The
change and the challenge are in many ways a mirror of the
challenge to Christianity itself in higher education.

Many chaplains have aspirations to become Scot Sloans,
but their actual jobs vary to such a degree that it is difficult
to say what exactly they are. The variations are endless. At
large schools that have a fair amount of religious participation, the chaplain's job is a full-time one; they conduct worship services, counsel and direct social service projects.
There the chaplain looks quite a bit like a parish minister. In
other schools, where you find a fulltime chaplain but little
religious interest, the chaplain is left to go scurrying around
simply in order to come up with projects "to pay the rent."

Other variations include chaplaincies with part-time teaching, and thus faculty status, or chaplaincies with part-time church relations work, that is, responsibility for maintaining and improving ties—including financial ones—with the affiliated denomination. Thus the importance of a chaplaincy varies from college to college, ranging from the prestigious "Dean of the Chapel" to a figurehead needed to keep whatever denominational money there is flowing and to be the official invoker of the deity at convocations.

Because the needs of any particular college vary so greatly with respect to its chaplaincy, there is little use in trying to give an ideal job description. What can and should be done, though, is to try to describe the importance of a chaplaincy to a college and so to evaluate some of the church's most vital tasks within higher education. The chaplain's calling centers around two challenges. First, it is to present alternatives, the alternatives that Christianity poses to the educational community. Second, it is to build up the community so that the hoped-for alternatives may be lived out. In times past both functions may very well have been filled by a ministry of social action and intellectual discernment that galvanized the whole community, and in some cases that continues. Where it does, the community is physician to its own health. Often, however, the community needs to be directly challenged; it does not have an adequate idea of what true health is, and has few resources within itself for a cure.

The problem is that educational communities are not always very aware of the needs of the whole person and often fail to meet them. They need to be awakened to what those needs are. If the real goal of education is that the student may learn to will a good life, then we cannot ignore the education of the will even though institutionally we are training the intellect. Although we cannot expect rigorous adherence to moral and doctrinal systems and still remain a school, we also cannot remain a school if we ignore or forget what and why we are teaching—that students may learn to shape their lives well. As John Henry Newman saw, if the community's actual practice runs contrary to leading a life for Christian ends, it does not matter what is taught or officially stated. In this regard the challenge to the educational community is one which seeks to coordinate what is lived on a daily basis with what is taught intellectually. Community life is essential to developing the whole person and vital to making a faith.

Often, however, the community life of colleges is not very healthy, despite being cited—particularly in the case of smaller schools—by many students as a reason for choosing a school. Yet there are no automatic advantages to a smaller school. Instead, as in any community, careful attention needs to be paid within these schools to developing a community where the whole person is educated, as well as to those factors which subvert community. Think of the ever-present problem on virtually every campus of "social excess" in the form of alcohol and recreational drugs. The life of liberal learning is always, I suspect, going to be accompanied by excess as young minds try out the limits of freedom. The problem is probably ineradicable and no school ought to delude itself that "it doesn't happen here." It does, and within some limits ought even to be tolerated.

Yet when a college has become a "party school," this is another matter entirely. When large parties are regularly scheduled on nights before classes and exams, the community is drifting towards gusto and not towards the formation of an adult character. When dorm life is consistently noisy and the bathrooms reek of stale beer and vomit, when student expectations are to "party" whenever possible, the development of a mature mind is almost impossible. Despite a school's stated intentions or even a faculty's genuine concern for the development of students, education is simply truncated. The message is heard, because it is lived out, that knowledge does not have any moral or religious context.

The chaplain ought to present a direct challenge to such a situation, even more so should it fall on deaf ears. The chal-

lenge, however, does not consist of measuring student behavior by rigid moral and doctrinal standards. Few things
could be less fruitful. Rather the challenge needs to be educational: behavior not only reflects values, it also creates them.
In this respect the challenge may very well be not a matter of
getting students to toe the line, but to ask for a reasonable
line. For example, many schools related to Christian
denominations have on their rule books a no-drinking policy,
but the policy is unenforced and regularly flouted. It may be
far better to ask for a more liberal policy, so that community
standards may be understood and lived, than to press for
abstinence. The belief that one standard does not really count
may lead to the belief that one can pick and choose standards
according to whim.

Social excess is a permanent topic of interest on campuses.
However, it poses less of a threat to the community than
another kind of excessive behavior: coercion and verbal
abuse. Such behavior does not involve the violation of rules,
yet it is perhaps even more destructive of the development of
a faith. Coercion consists of acts that do not involve physical
force, but are just as effective in intimidating and violating
others. They are acts which violate integrity, forcing others
into a mold and a way of thinking they might be too frightened
to resist. This violation is perhaps even more destructive of
education and Christian purposes than the guns which appeared on so many campuses in the sixties and of which Allan
Bloom makes so much in his book.

One example that comes to mind of this sort of violence
took place at a college talent show. A young woman, a good
singer, did a striking bluesy rendition of George Gershwin's
"Summertime." Despite the fact that her act was clearly the
best thing in a show that otherwise tended to the moronic and
inept, her performance was received with hoots of derision.
To her great credit she finished the performance. But what
were the results? She was utterly humiliated in front of her
family and friends, a humiliation taken so to heart that she

withdrew from school at the end of the semester. The long-term result, however, may have been worse; it is doubtful that she will ever do anything like that again. And even if she *were* to perform again, the message was clear to everyone: "Don't be different or try to excel. If you do, you will be punished." That message goes beyond mere performance; it enforces and mandates a certain sort of average behavior in almost everything.

The school at which this happened is not unique. When I told this story to my father, the light of recognition dawned in his eyes, for he grew up in a small town and had ambitions larger than the town. Apparently there were yahoos there, too. It is no surprise that he, like many people who come from small towns, have never looked back after leaving them.

This is one example of what sort of behavior needs to be challenged. There are others as well, since often *any* difference is enough to invoke persecution. Sexual and racial differences are favorite targets. One dean of students related a story of two gay students who felt so threatened by their fellow students in a conservative midwestern college that they did not return after one semester. In that case the threats were physical but they also included name-calling, with the tag homosexual, a tag that can keep one from doing things he might otherwise do that might benefit the community. Similarly, many campuses have reported ugly racial incidents in recent years as part of a continuing undercurrent of racism. As many Black educators have pointed out, Black students rarely fare very well under those circumstances, since their experience leads them to understand a subtle message that they are not expected to succeed. As a result they have begun to return to Black colleges, where the explicit message is, "You can succeed."

These examples are enough to arouse the righteous indignation of liberals, and rightly so. The same sort of problem, however, can occur in schools that are not considered provincial at all and have thorough-going liberal credentials.

Speakers for unpopular conservative causes have been kept out of such schools, as Jeane Kirkpatrick was at Harvard several years ago. Students and faculty who have expressed reservation over issues like divestment in South Africa are often too easily tagged as "soft on racism." Divestment may very well be the right thing to do, but the issue is a complex one and cannot be solved by slogans and stereotyping of positions. Slogans and stereotypes are a poor way to decide any issue; educationally, it is disastrous to exert group pressure on individual minds.

All of these examples involve non-physical violence. All of them involve some kind of abuse; all violate persons in one way or another. How? They do so in a twofold way, for they involve the violation of personal integrity and the debasement of the common good.

Those who have been on the receiving end of mocking, threats or name-calling feel they have been violated just as surely as if they were beaten up. To be violated means that your sense of being worthwhile is lost, to be replaced by a sense counting for little except as an object of ridicule. This sense of violation and of ensuing worthlessness is disastrous for people in the eighteen to twenty-two year old age group, who are only beginning to develop a sense of self worth and security. To go through an experience like this tends to confirm one's worst self-doubts. It would be nice if we could simply counsel people in situations like this to be courageous, but unfortunately to be courageous one needs to feel secure in something. Mocking, name calling and social ostracism are a quick way to destroy courage. Worse yet, once students lose their sense of security and courage, they easily join the persecuting group and imitate its behavior in order to be accepted and feel secure once again. This, I suspect, is the reason for fraternity hazing. Feelings of worthlessness are intensified in cases of non-physical abuse, since there is little recourse. If you are mugged, you can at least get revenge by calling the police and initiating a suit; there is nothing you can do when you have been verbally abused.

Such violence is a community problem. It kills the initiative badly needed by the community through killing of self-esteem. Without initiative, personal differences tend to be leveled and an overall mediocrity, liberal or conservative, is enforced. When this sort of violence becomes common, the general level of thought and culture is *never* raised; it is only lowered. When nobody dares to be different, the lowest common denominator itself goes still lower. Few things are more antithetical to the educational process or to making a faith, both meant to free the individual and contribute to the common good, than coercion.

Of course it is difficult to draw the line. When is non-physical force excessive and when is it not? You cannot expect anybody—much less college students of spirit—always to speak gently and in an edifying manner. But the problem isn't where to draw the line; it lies in permitting an atmosphere where students expect to be undermined or assaulted in some way for trying to excel, to be different. Although I have used examples of gross social persecution, the same point ought to be taken in regard to intellectual and religious opinion. One is not going to learn a faith simply by living in a polite community, of course, but it is decidedly difficult to learn it when one is mocked for it. In this regard, colleges have to see their mission in moral education extending into the realm of communal behavior.

College chaplains have to raise these issues. To be sure, any member of a healthy community ought to raise them and evince concern as to how communal life affects education, yet the chaplain as a minister of the gospel of reconciliation must have a special concern. He needs to raise the issue in a way that links the fundamental ends of human life, the importance of education, and the formation community. It is not enough to be content with a community that merely tolerates study; a desire for education should permeate communal life. In this way, the chaplain's job is still analogous to her duties in former and more active times. During the 1960s the Christian commitment was not simply to eradicate racism or cause withdrawal from an unjust war, it was to establish a just society. Today it is not simply a matter of getting rid of misguided behavior so that students may make free choices, but of trying to articulate what to do with that freedom. Where there are forces working against that freedom they need to be challenged. One writer on liberal education, Christopher Derrick, succinctly notes: "A liberal education can educate the young *for* freedom, if it knows what human freedom is and what it's for: it will deprive them grievously if it tries too simply to educate them *by means of* freedom."[13]

In recent years the American theological ethicist, Stanley Hauerwas, has made a great deal of the idea that morality is a function of character and that character depends upon the communities in which we live. He also argues that the Christian community, the body of Christ, must be a community in which its members experience the confidence of grace to such a degree that they can tell the truth about themselves. Hauerwas' points may easily be applied to the Christian liberal arts colleges in order to suggest how they may contribute to the life of faith. Although they are not churches, they should still be communities where a Christian character can be formed by accepting the truth without fear of reprisals. This includes both the intellect and social life. If you are going to belong to the "body," you need to know the truth about it and you must be able to live it. A chaplain's challenge to the college community is to become a community where the truth may be lived, and not merely talked about.

That challenge oftentimes needs to be extended beyond students themselves and directed at administrations and administrators. For example, one form of coercion perpetuated by administrators is the failure to hear what people are really going through in their college life and so to tackle communal problems. Take the problem of abusive behavior, with its victims' ensuing feelings of worthlessness. These feelings can be compounded when it seems there is nothing that can or will be done about it; the student feels totally impotent. When schools don't listen to these complaints, when they tolerate an atmosphere in which people are abused, then in a sense the administration adds to the violence. A victim's sense of unfair treatment is hard enough; the realization that what has happened to him is not important enough to do anything about—or even to prevent in the future—is even harder.

Educational institutions are natural institutions, subject to natural necessities and pressures. Nothing guarantees their permanent validity or even their survival. As in other institutions, truthfulness can often play a secondary role to more pragmatic concerns of survival and prestige. Thus schools can be reluctant to change social life on campus, even when in the long run it is of no help to the student, for fear of offending students and losing the constituency they enjoy. Or they may be reluctant to change because change would constitute an admission that something is not exactly right. Thus even schools which portray themselves as Christian liberal arts colleges may tend to undermine that identity, becoming increasingly vocational in order to cater to student whims. Or they may refuse to confront the hard task of reevaluating the curriculum and everybody's comfortable position in the *status quo*. Or, if they have gained a certain degree of academic prestige, they may quietly let any kind of Christian identity lapse, slip away unnoticed, to be dragged out and dusted off for contributors who are interested in that sort of thing. The drive for security by the increasing of the endowment can leave a school rudderless, as chief administrative officers spend more time courting donors and less in educating. In all these cases, if the school is to fulfill a Christian end, it must be reawakened to a Christian alternative.

It is a chaplain's duty to present that challenge and to do that awakening. When there is trouble in student life, this may mean offering guidance and compassion. Yet just as often it may not be the students who need to be challenged, but the administration and faculty. Situations may come about where a chaplain's contribution to a school may involve very little contact with students, but a great deal of work with those who direct the curriculum and student affairs. The chaplain's job is an educational one; it cannot be evaluated on the model of a parish pastor. While both may be counselors and comforters, even prophets, the pastor is guiding and counseling people who have decided to belong to a community. The chaplain, on the other hand, usually has to be the one who brings community issues to the attention of students, faculty and administrators. Furthermore, rarely does the chaplain have a natural community—she will be as concerned about Catholics and Jews as she is about Protestants, and vice versa. She will rarely have any prescribed authority beyond the authority of the Gospel and sacraments. Even that authority will not always be decisive; the community she belongs to will always include those who do not recognize it.

A school's Christian commitment can be measured at times by the degree to which it is open to the voice of challenge. No school is without its problems. Even returning seminary alumni often remark on how much present student complaints about the "lack of community" resemble their own in the past. A truly excellent school is one that insists those voices be heard, giving them both opportunity and status. By contrast, think of the schools that deliberately hire chaplains without giving them faculty status. Such chaplains are rarely heard, not only because they cannot make motions in a faculty meeting, but also because Ph.D.s seldom listen to those who are not of their own kind. In many cases, a school that deliberately withholds status has already decided it does not need an alternative point of view, at least not Christianity's. In institutions where status means so much, to withhold it, or to refrain from seeking chaplains who have those credentials is to regard the job as insignificant.

A great sense of excitement and virtue always accompanies any vocation that takes the risk of challenging systems; the chaplaincy is no exception. Such a sense must have been a great motivation in campus ministry some years ago, when great and dramatic challenges were directed to the larger society. However, in a time when the challenge is issued from *within* to the community itself such a risk can lead to a feeling that one is living the life of the prophet Jeremiah. While refusing to leave Jerusalem even when it was on the verge of destruction, Jeremiah spent the larger portion of his prophetic ministry challenging that community to return and realize its intended destiny. His personal reward was to be mocked, ignored, seen as a cranky doomsayer. The prophet wished he had never responded to his call. In much the same way a chaplaincy can lead to frustration and a sense of being irrelevant.

This sense of frustration is hardly unique to a chaplain; campuses are full of professors who wish they were taken more seriously. However, a chaplain's frustration is often played out quite differently. For the chaplain who is trying to awake a college to a sense of community, who is trying to provide an example of how to live, frustration may lead to confusion, capitulation to unhealthy communal norms or, on the other hand, to angry contrariness.

A chaplain can articulate a very clear sense of how a community ought to look, of its underlying raison d'etre, and still be misunderstood. One chaplain, for example, spoke about working in a school where alcohol was forbidden yet enforcement so lax that, despite the policy, alcohol abuse was common among students. Now my friend had a very clear sense of how alcohol ought to be used within the college. He believed that students, if they were going to drink, ought to be allowed—and expected—to do so in a adult way. The no-alcohol policy, he thought, only encouraged habits usually associated with drinking in the back seats of cars. However, his suggestions to change the policy were heard by the president as opening the door to the school becoming an "animal house"—although it already was. Students, on the other hand, saw his refusal to drink with them while the policy was in effect as middle-aged prudishness.

Frustration, and the high degree of freedom found in academic communities, can also lead chaplains to give up presenting any real alternatives. Instead, they try to excel at the very things to which they are supposed to provide alternatives. One chaplain at a prestigious college explained how demanding her job was in view of the fact that she had to commute every weekend to a town three hours away where her husband and young child lived. Clearly she was inviting sympathy and could build a case for herself as an adult role model, since many of her students would find themselves in similar situations shortly after graduation. But what alternatives was she really giving them? She had fully accepted the role of "Successful Mother-cum-Career-Woman," a role that would eat up many of her students in the future. Furthermore, whatever she might have to say about community life has a hollow ring since she could and did walk away from it every weekend. At the same time she was undoubtedly extolling the virtues of community and the sacrifices necessary to maintain it, she simply was not available to the community twenty-five percent of the time. Nor was she available to her other community—her family—seventy-five percent of the time. Of course the problem was not hers alone. Her husband, also a minister, couldn't give up his church to move closer to her work.

At the other extreme is the chaplain who has capitulated to nothing. He is quite sure of what alternatives students, faculty and administrators need. He may even be right, but frustration has led to anger and because of that anger, he can see little good within his community. At this point his commitment may become self-destructive; it may even create further communal problems. One wag once noted that faculty politics are especially dirty since the stakes are small and the egos so big. Pressing unpopular issues with a sense of isolated self-righteousness only adds one more big ego.

Frustration is the constant shadow of a chaplain's job; since it involves criticism and confrontation, frustration inevitably arises. Yet it need not be destructive. Criticism and confrontation are not the only ways of raising alternatives; alternatives can also be brought to light by encouraging them whenever they exist. When a chaplain encourages people with good ideas, she is not shouldering the burden of moral leadership alone—she is playing the role of a community member. The all-important job of counseling is an example of this. To be sure, pastoral counseling is a matter of healing wounds, but it is healing through sharing that person's life. The satisfaction of helping another is not merely the satisfaction of a job well-done; it is the satisfaction of true communal life where, as St. Paul said: "If one member suffers, all suffer together; if one member is honored, all rejoice together." (I Cor. 12.26)

Challenging unreflective popular opinion is part of a chaplain's most routine duty, conducting worship. I noted earlier that religion is not simply a theory of human origins—it is a lived reality. Therefore it cannot simply be learned in a classroom. Church-related schools have a unique resource in their ongoing programs of chapel worship and fellowship groups, for in such programs is the opportunity to live the real thing and not just talk about it. In a similar way, campus ministries at state universities also provide perhaps the only opportunity students at those institutions have for developing faith.

There is a real analogy between a college chapel program and a scientific laboratory course. In laboratory courses students do not simply mix chemicals chaotically and without supervision. Instead, what experiments they do are highly deliberate; the professor tries to impress upon the student how scientific method "feels" in its execution by duplicating classic experiments and discoveries. The results are not supposed to be chaotic; indeed, they are well-defined ahead of time. By carefully directing a student through experiments, they can reach those results themselves.

The same thing might be said of chapel worship. Unlike the formal worship of a congregation, it can be an experiment in faith. This is not to say that college worship should be bizarre, in an effort to attract otherwise uninterested students; it is to point out that it can be, and within colleges ought to be, educational. It is the teaching of the Christian alternative through a lived, and shared, experience. Within the few minutes of common worship, a student is learning to share her faith with others she may not have known before. Through worship she may find increasing mutuality and depth in understanding with these companions. She has the chance to experiment with attitudes and to talk about them openly. In most colleges, she will even have the opportunity to structure and lead worship and, quite literally, to experiment with it.

College worship also has the possibility of being a laboratory for the entire college community; it can be a source for further growth. It is usually informal; it can afford to include on a regular basis, and in some depth, issues of science and social life. The programs and topics we have presented and discussed in the Illinois College chapel in the last few years, for example, have included panel discussions and programs on racism, abortion, date rape, personal and family violence, alcoholism and communal morale. Outside speakers have addressed such issues as international relations, nuclear disarmament, women and religion, education, science and religion and contemporary theological and biblical issues. This sampling is fairly typical. The point of these programs is not strictly informational, nor are they meant to be simply academic exercises; they are a way of building bridges between faith and the world in which it dwells, so that faith may be a living option in the life of students and faculty.

Chapel worship can, therefore, be an extremely important part of the life of a college. There faith is simply not exempted from reflection and critical study, nor is any part of academic life exempted from critical reflection. Worship provides education with a goal and context: what is learned in college is brought to bear upon worship, while worship extends a challenge to how one views the ends of education. Thus a church-related college can be a community in which investigation is truly free and open, without ceasing to be a place in which experience is lived experience—lived in the light of what is ultimate.

These suggestions about the value of communal worship within the college community are undoubtedly idealistic. Student interest in voluntary chapel at many schools is not high; compulsory chapel services are resisted to such an extent that they become disruptive. For my part, I offer silent thanks to a predecessor who was instrumental in removing the chapel attendance requirement since it simply offered the powers that be a weekly chance to hector the faculty and students. Now, although attendance is small, there is nevertheless a genuine attitude of worship.

Idealistic or not, these suggestions can serve at least three purposes. First, they emphasize to the schools themselves the importance of worship and fellowship groups in the education of students, and so deserve the full commitment of the institution. Second, they point to the all-important aspect of community, especially a worshipping community, in developing the whole person. If communal worship is the religious equivalent of the laboratory, then the communal life of any campus (including the chapel) is the laboratory of the whole person. Finally, chaplains *can* present alternative choices to a community through encouraging and developing those alternatives which already exist.

It is too easy simply to criticize communities; criticism has authenticity, however, only when the critic stands fully committed. Otherwise it is the criticism of the uprooted person who has never lived out what he preaches. A professor I once knew, when asked to join a student protest during the sixties,

said in all seriousness that he would be glad to help pull the
school down—if the students would help him rebuild it. He
knew the school's serious flaws, but he also knew very well
the school's important role in creating values with which to
protest.

There is a good biblical precedent for this professor's
belief. When Jerusalem was besieged by the armies of
Nebuchadrezzar, the prophet Jeremiah purchased property in
the town as a sign of the fact that it would be reestablished.
He did this despite the fact that he had previously severely
criticized the people of Jerusalem for violence and idolatry,
and warned them of the consequences. When everybody else
fled, Jeremiah chose to stay and was removed from the ruined
town only by force. Jeremiah criticized Jerusalem when it for-
got its real call. In doing so he clearly implies its value, a
value to which in the end he was willing to commit his life.

Here is another example, drawn from the stories of the
prophet Elijah. During the idolatrous reign of King Ahab in
Israel, Elijah challenged the priests of Baal to a contest on
Mount Carmel; the outcome would prove whether Baal or
Yahweh was truly God. When Elijah won, he righteously slew
five hundred priests of Baal. Thus he made his critical point.
Elijah's job was not finished, however, as he understood very
well when Jezebel, the queen, informed him that he would die
if he were caught inside Israel. And so he fled to Mount Sinai
believing that he alone in all of Israel was faithful to Yahweh.
Undoubtedly he was frustrated and in despair; even after his
astounding victory on Carmel, nobody seemed to be listening. On Mount Sinai, however, Yahweh revealed to him that
he, Yahweh, had saved seven thousand in Israel who had not
bowed the knee to Baal. These were to be the core of the re-
establishment of Israel; Elijah and his successor Elisha were
to gather them together.

While the dramatic action of slaying the priests of Baal
might have been necessary, by itself it did not establish the
alternative Elijah wanted for Israel. That alternative could

only be established through all those whom Yahweh, and not Elijah, had saved for the job. It was only through the people as a whole, and not through the action of a lone gun, that the community was going to be reestablished.

How do these Old Testament stories shed light on a chaplain's vocation? While there are indeed times that criticism, even harsh and rigorous criticism, must be directed at institutions that have worshipped prestige and pandered to contentment (slaying the administration, however, may be a bit extreme) criticism is still only half the job. The other, and perhaps more important, half is to give yourself to the community. Like Jeremiah, a chaplain needs to issue criticism from a sense of the deep importance of the community; she must also find signs of hope within it. Like Elijah, a chaplain needs to find, encourage and gather together those who are the real future of the community. Never can her criticism be that of a mere observer.

This question of combining criticism with dedication raises one final aspect of the chaplain's vocation, the commitment to social activism. Just as there is danger in criticizing a school without being committed to it, so too there is a danger of promoting activism without spiritual roots. Criticism without a strong commitment to what is being criticized—the body—is rootless activism. Social action is crucial to developing a faith because our God is a God of justice. At a time when either the wind has gone out of the sails of activism or activism has lost its religious dimension at many colleges, the "inner," contemplative side of activism needs further attention.

In the medieval church, the story of Jesus' encounter with the sisters Mary and Martha symbolized the two separate forms of religious vocation. Hardworking Martha symbolized the active life in this world; Mary stood for the contemplative life. It was to Mary that Jesus assigned the "better portion." In turn, theology assigned the better portion to monks and nuns who devoted themselves strictly to contemplative pursuits. Contemporary theologians argue that the story deals with the primacy of faith and with the need to have faith in order that works of service not become hollow. This story of the primacy of faith is intended, we are told, to provide a balance to the story of the Good Samaritan's works, a story which immediately precedes this one in the Gospel of Luke. The story of Mary and Martha does not justify a separate and "higher" form of life known as the contemplative, for in balancing it with that of the Good Samaritan, Jesus commends the active life to all all Christians.

Unfortunately the contemporary interpretation commending the active life may have forgotten that action needs to be balanced by contemplation, that contemplation is also commended. When contemplation, or the aspect of faith that thrives on it, is ignored then there is no balance to a life lived by works alone. And where there is no such balance, the energy for necessary works dissipates.

During the sixties there was on American campuses an intense concern for social justice. Part of this concern manifested itself in rebellion against the Vietnam War; some of it appeared in the efforts to eradicate racism and economic oppression. This concern for social justice was not merely secular humanism and liberal outrage. Many of the people who worked hardest for justice were Christians, including chaplains, and their heroes were Martin Luther King and Dietrich Bonhoeffer, their theorists theologians such as the Niebuhrs and Paul Tillich. It seemed to many people at the time that we were indeed loving God through serving our brothers and sisters.

A number of years have passed since the heyday of this movement and the rule of social justice it sought has not been established. What is of equally grave concern now is the spirit that characterizes activist causes, which oscillates between somnolence and chaos. On some campuses there is simple indifference, if not hostility, to these causes. On others, some form of social activism continues, although often in reduced numbers and often without any sort of coherence. Feminist causes, South African disvestment, racism, and Central America, to name just a few of the movements, do not always coalesce. There does not seem to be a guiding vision. What is true of campuses also seems to be true in many churches. Even where activism is strong and alive, a bystander can easily receive the impression that everybody is pressing their own cause as the most important. Righteous indignation persists, but that is not enough.

What has brought this about? Perhaps the oft-repeated suggestion that students are more concerned about security and jobs is correct, but only to a degree. What we lack is the necessary vision and spirit, a spirit that is only present when we contemplate the source of justice, as Mary contemplated Jesus' words. There is an unbreakable and essential connection between action and contemplation. But as the gospel shows, there is also a certain priority to contemplation, a priority which is meant to give both spirit and meaning to action. Earlier, I mentioned one chaplain who led students in social causes but was never able to speak to them in chapel because they weren't there. Since he felt he could not solve the problem by himself, he left the chaplaincy for a parish that had its spiritual house in order and now wanted to begin an energetic program of outreach. He understood the point of the Mary and Martha story.

College chaplains have a unique opportunity to offer a coherent vision to their communities. The uniqueness, however, does not simply lie in the content of that vision, important though it is. It lies also in the opportunity, through worship and reflection, to tap the springs of the Spirit in order to bring that vision about. Social action is crucial, especially for students who are beginning their adult lives and need to learn to lead them responsibly. We serve students well by directing them to these activities. But at the same time we also have the opportunity to serve them as our neighbors—letting them see for themselves the value of contemplation and teach them its ways and means. And if we do, we will give to them the better portion and one not to be taken from them.

Chapter Seven

Apostles, Prophets, Teachers

Truth is often stranger than fiction, especially when one is dealing with students. Consider the following story: A professor of religion at a midwestern Presbyterian college was teaching a ten lecture unit on the New Testament in a religion course required of all sophomore students. Of these ten lectures he spent two days discussing the idea of the kingdom of God, because, as he observed to his students, it is the thing Jesus talked about most. At the end of the unit the professor conducted a review session, which he opened by asking the single question, "What does Jesus talk about most?" Yet instead of being met with a chorus of "The kingdom of God!" all he got was stony silence. When he told his students that this wouldn't do, that he had stressed this in lectures, one young woman raised her hand and bravely replied, "We should believe in him."

The professor went on to say that this student was not only a superior student, but a faithful member of the local Presbyterian church, a church in which he knew the pastor was not saying anything any different than he was. Furthermore when he checked the student's notebook he saw that she had reproduced the lectures extremely accurately. What then caused her answer?

Undoubtedly numerous cultural factors interfered with her ability to hear what was being said to her. Perhaps the dor-

mitory claptrap, which talks about religion as mere belief in
authority for a future payoff, caused her to assume that Jesus
must have been saying something of that kind. Since she was
a good notetaker, she may very well have been the sort of person who believes that knowledge is a matter of accepting
authority. When she heard and read shallow characterizations
of Christianity as being a matter of submitting to Jesus'
authority, she naively accepted them. She was misled about
religion, as many students are, and her remarks clearly show
this.

It is, however, too facile simply to blame her cultural en-
vironment, although it probably had a great deal to do with
her answer. Her remarks reveal something far deeper. Very
possibly she may not have regarded the church as the place
to gain information, which is to say that her roots in it did not
go very deep. The professor who told this story suggested that
mainline Protestant churches may be responsible for this root-
lessness—it is correlated with the collapse of their youth
movements. It may also be the case that the church itself was
not doing a very good job of teaching her the difference between true and false ideas about Christianity, perhaps because
it was confused itself. In either case she was not being educated very well by her church, nor is she unique, as I can well
attest. In teaching a course on "Basic Questions of the Christian Faith" each semester, I ask the class if they know what
the Trinity is. Despite the fact that the majority have a church
background of some kind, eighty percent do not know. Although the future adult members of churches ought to know
who God is, they are not finding it out.

When the faithful have ceased to know the tradition they
will cease to feel any identification with it. For its own survival, therefore, the church must involve itself deeply with
education at all levels. It must include education for adults
and children within the local church itself, and, just as important, the education of the clergy as well as the college educa-

tion of the laity. As one college president succinctly put it, the church needs to think of itself as having a ministry *of* education, rather than the present ministry *to* education.

Why should the church worry about the Christian education of adults both within and without the congregation? In the first place, very simply, adult lives need to be formed by the Christian story at an adult level. Psalm 78 tells of how God has established a testimony and law in Israel which he commanded our forebears to teach to their children, who would teach them to their children so, it is said, "that they should set their hope in God...and keep his commandments." That this is not just a matter for children has been well understood in orthodox Judaism, where adults spend enormous amounts of time studying the Torah. Many Christians, however, treat it as something that need not go beyond a childish understanding. George Bernanos once told the story of a village priest who candidly told his spiritual aspirations to the aristocratic baron living in the chateau overlooking the village. When he finished, the baron simply observed that he, too, had felt that way—when he was twelve years old. The young priest thought to himself, that is the way many people to think of faith, something childish that never need go beyond childhood.[14]

Unless people are taught at levels that go beyond their confirmation classes in the eighth or ninth grade, their understanding of the story will remain at the level of an eighth or ninth grader. The fact that the religious education of most people stops there undoubtedly explains in good part the popularity of "children's sermons" among the adult congregation; children themselves are relatively indifferent to the practice. We would be appalled if the voting population of the country decided major state and federal issues with only that level of education, yet somehow we have not seen this as much of a problem in the church. For this reason alone the church needs to put its hand to higher education.

What does it take to educate Christians at an adult level? In the first place, it takes giving them knowledge of the biblical story at a level where they can realize that Christian faith requires more of us than "that we should believe in him." Few lives are so lacking in complexity that a single motto will suffice to hold them together and give them purpose. The Bible, however, is not a single motto; it is witness to the faith of many different people whose lives were just as complex as ours, whose lives changed as often as ours. The way these people dealt with their lives and the "various and many ways that God spoke to them in the past" (Hebrews 1.1) is crucial to understanding what God has revealed in Christ. Without knowledge of the story in its complexity, faith is simply simple-minded.

There is another reason, beyond the personal, why teaching the Christian story is important. The knowledge and commitment to the story which the church shares is what makes it a community, a body. Adult faith is to a very great extent shared faith, even if it is held individually. The story of faith, whether we are talking about Israel, the disciples learning from Jesus, or the squabbles in the Corinthian church, is the story of a community; it is also the basis for a living community, the church now. Just as I suggested in an earlier chapter that schools, when really educating the whole person, are not merely imparting information but introducing students into the larger body of culture, so too the church's education introduces its members into a larger body. The church is not a community, a body, that exists because of cosy agapes; it exists as a community because of commonly held ideals and an understanding of what is possible to achieve them. In short, it is community of common knowledge and tradition, bound together by grace.

For the church, the most important aspect of its common tradition is the biblical story; it is not the only one, however. The "cloud of witnesses" does not end with the apostles, it continues on to the present day and includes Augustine,

Aquinas, Luther, Calvin, and Bonhoeffer. These witnesses and countless others are crucial for *how* we read the biblical story and for how we live it. The Protestant principle of "sola scriptura" often obscures this, yet a tradition of interpretation functions in important ways even in Protestant churches. The mere fact that they say the Apostles' Creed demonstrates this. The Creed is not the result of a committee's decision about what Christians ought to believe; it enshrines the interpretation of Jesus' words given by those to whom he entrusted those words. By reciting it we join Augustine, Aquinas, Luther and Calvin, and the Apostles, in a community of common understanding of Jesus' teaching and life. It is a means by which we claim the Bible as our common story and subsequently claim each other.

Knowledge and use of the continuing tradition is important to churches in order to be a community, a community of those present and those past. Adult faith requires acquaintance with this tradition. Without it, the task of preaching would require extensive proof-texting each Sunday; with it, pastors may rely on the possession of common goals and expectations shared by their hearers and themselves. They may appeal to this common understanding, this communal sense, to charge a congregation or to deepen their appreciation of their task.

Unless one is living within a sect, cut off from the rest of the culture, however, this common frame of reference will also include aspects of the larger culture, such as science and politics and literature. In the end the preacher must focus *both* a biblical tradition and a tradition of common understanding that has developed alongside it. Or, more accurately, the preacher must be able to focus a single tradition which combines the biblical story and the elements of the broader culture in such a way that the community will remain faithful to the biblical story.

This is an immense—if not impossible—task for a single hour on Sunday morning unless one can rely upon a congregation that is educated in the essentials of Christian and cultural

life. When a congregation already has an educated sense of
both the Gospel and the world, this focusing is not only possible it is highly effective. A community that is aware of its
roots is one that can hear, and even anticipate, the message.
One that is unaware will, in Isaiah's words, hear and hear
again, but not hear. For this reason both education within the
church and higher education is critical to the church's well-
being.

Yet this ideal situation does not occur very often. The
reason is not that the ideal is too high—it does not require a
congregation of nuclear physicists well versed in patristics—
but that it is seldom even recognized as an ideal. Instead of
seeking a community of shared knowledge, the church, like
the university, has invested its knowledge in what it thinks
are experts—the clergy.

Consider for a moment the reaction of a supposedly well
educated, middle-class congregation to two sermons
preached by its long time pastor. In the first, he preached on
the Parable of the Vineyard (Matthew 21.33–46). It is the
story of a landowner who rents his vineyard to people who
refuse to pay the rent and, in order to seize the land for themselves, beat the owner's servants and finally kill his son when
they were sent to collect the rent. The parable is intended as
an allegory of Jesus' hostile reception by the world. However,
by a miracle of exegesis, the pastor concluded by coming
squarely down on the side of the tenants of the vineyard. Although I am not sure of how he did it, apparently he took the
owner of the vineyard to be a first century slumlord, and his
servants and son a strongarmed collection agency. What was
interesting about the sermon was less its exegesis, though,
than the reaction of the congregation or, rather, its lack of any
reaction at all. No one blinked an eye. Two weeks later,
however, when the pastor preached a sermon which suggested
that Christians might have some interest in peace and justice
in Central America, members of the congregation were in

paroxysms of righteous indignation for the better part of a month.

The reactions of this congregation illustrate very well how the clergy have come to be regarded as "experts" and "professionals." The first sermon, which was essentially the exposition of a biblical text, could not be criticized. Expounding the Bible is entirely within the purview of the minister's professional tasks. Like a doctor or lawyer, he was an authority to be listened to. If you did not like what was being said, of course, you might seek another professional for a second opinion, but you would not question the expertise—especially if you had no knowledge about the subject yourself. In the second sermon, however, the minister was clearly perceived as having stepped out of the unassailable role of expert and therefore could be criticized at will. Yet knowledge still played no role here; the message was biblically sound, but criticized nonetheless.

What this example typifies is the ever-widening gap between the clergy and laity in most mainline Protestant denominations. The clergy are regarded as experts—and to a certain degree they are. By having accepted higher biblical criticism, mainline Protestantism has developed a fairly complex and subtle understanding of the Bible. Hence it does take time and effort to train the clergy. Where the problem lies is with the minister's use of sophisticated critical techniques, or results derived from them, in order to preach to a congregation that does not have the faintest notion of how and why these conclusions about the Bible have been reached. So to adopt the ready-to-hand model of proclaiming the minister an expert seems the simplest and wisest course. Of course it is also self-defeating, for at that point the gap between the clergy and laity widens even further. What mainline Protestantism attempts to be in the modern world in good part depends on biblical criticism, but it also depends upon the participation of the laity. It seems, then, that mainline Protestantism has gotten itself into a difficult dilemma. Going back to the story with which I began, no wonder that the student could not hear what the professor was saying; they were in different worlds.

The problem is an educational issue, for its roots lie in ignorance. Education is the means by which the values of a tradition are transmitted to a new generation and the new generation is claimed by this tradition. Using this definition, what kind of transmitting and claiming actually occurs?

Within the public schools there is, of course, little transmission of the Christian tradition. Higher public education that sails under the flag of "academic freedom" does no better. If students attend state universities, there is virtually no chance within the university itself for them to deepen their knowledge of Christianity. Furthermore, they will probably be under little or no pressure to come to some sort of coherent vision of their world and culture; instead, they will be pressured to choose a major and prepare themselves for a job. In their turn, students demand this kind of training. If they attend a liberal arts college, even one that is church-related, given the mood of the present student population they will also be searching for vocational preparation. At the end of either education, they will probably know nothing more about Christianity than when they began. Even for those students who by virtue of some form of church education have come to some knowledge of the Bible, it is not likely that they will possess any knowledge of the classical writings of Christianity or a sense of Christianity itself as a living tradition. When they return to the pews of their local churches, they will know little more than when they left—if they return at all.

This situation leaves the greater part of educating Christians in the hands of the churches. The task is one of the whole church, including the laity. Nevertheless a major portion of its oversight falls to the clergy; not because they are educational "experts," but because they are the ones who by virtue of their own education should have the most accurate sense of all that the task involves. They are, after all, the ones who have to focus the biblical and cultural traditions each Sunday. Yet how good is the education of the clergy?

Unfortunately, the news is not good. The undergraduate education of clergy is hardly different than that of the laity. Many clergy have been educated in state universities; few, as under graduates, take many courses in religion. This is particularly true as vocations to the ordained ministry are increasing for men and women who are some years out of college. Educationally this means they begin their seminary education with the level of Christian knowledge that they had as seniors in high school. It is ironic that at the very time seminaries began admitting large numbers of students with narrow and non-theological backgrounds, they also upgraded the title of the basic divinity degree from a bachelor's to a master's.

The Episcopal Church has recently suggested that instead of waiting for people with vocations to approach the church, the church ought to be actively seeking out qualified people. It is an important suggestion; nevertheless the Christian ministry is not and cannot be confined to those who have received a call at the same time they are registering for undergraduate courses. Seminaries certainly recognize this; to a great degree, they attempt to provide an education that in certain ways is a more thorough and specific equivalent of the liberal arts religion major. Seminary students are given broad exposure to the terrain of theological knowledge with some eye to broader application. Even here, though, there are problems. First, as Edward Farley has argued, a "professional model" of theological education tends to dominate seminaries. Consequently students are given an education that is as narrowly skill-oriented as any undergraduate's. Students seem to accept this whole-heartedly; hence those courses which do not appear to be immediately useful in professional life—such as Hebrew and Greek—are merely tolerated, without planting any seeds that will develop into habits of thought.

Second, this tendency to make seminary education into a skill-oriented "professional" one is reinforced by the sketchy background in religious thought that many seminarians have at the time of matriculation. Because they have studied little or no philosophy, for example, any deep understanding of writers such as Augustine or Aquinas or Schleiermacher is usually beyond them. Seminaries rarely attempt to remedy this. According to the Association of Theological Schools, the number of faculty responsible for teaching philosophy in seminaries has declined from fifty-five in 1967—itself a desparately low number—to thirty-five in 1977, with further declines since then. The issue is not so much philosophy per se, but access to the history of Christian theology. It is small wonder that few ministers take more than the required number of courses in theology proper, and fewer read much in it after seminary.

The outlook for biblical studies is similarly depressing. A seminary classmate of mine once complained bitterly of being required to learn Hebrew and Greek. He insisted that commentaries are so good and so numerous nowadays that the depths of biblical exegesis have become accessible to any minister. By the end of his seminary career, however, my classmate had made only the feeblest start on acquiring a commentary on each book of the Bible, much less the two or three he would really need. He had also deprived himself of deeper understanding of language itself that Greek or Hebrew provides, hence affecting his ability to deal with written texts. He, like so many other future clergy, hid himself in courses in counseling and administration techniques and homiletics because they were "useful."

What does this mean for seminary graduates? They enter parishes as professionals and that is how they continue to view themselves, thus holding firmly onto the professional model. Ironically, within the parish they are regarded as experts in the same theological disciplines and biblical studies that they tried to avoid in seminary! Of course this is easy to do in a congregation of uninformed laity that simply acquiesces in the myth of expertise. In time, even the clergy begin to believe they are experts, especially after they gain acess to a Doctor of Ministry program. While numerous clergy have become better ministers through such programs, many of their professors are agreed that the main attraction of these programs does not seem to be educational; it lies in gaining a degree which increases the possible advance of its owner to a larger congregation.

There is undoubtedly something very unfair about this picture if it is taken as a characterization of the clergy as unlettered and uninterested. It would be a mere caricature. The fact of the matter is that most clergy are caring and dedicated people. Yet for reasons often beyond their control, their educational background is not all that it could be; theology, rather than being a practiced means of making the historical body come alive, remains a matter of some discomfort and mystery for many clergy. This is not simply a lack of scholarly preparation; it also reaches back into the style of their collegiate education. Where there has been no recognition of the moral or historical and cultural context of education—no sense of *paideia*—it is difficult for them to pick this up in seminary or to teach it within the community of the church in the world. If the diversity of knowledge has not been focused in their education, so that they may feel that they are part of a larger body, it is difficult for them to focus it for others. Many ministers soon recognize a problem like this as they become concerned with developing a common frame of meaning in a church. Unfortunately, they often need to start figuring out how to do this from scratch within a parish, or else they have to turn to some expert to learn a technique on how to do it. So it is increasingly difficult for them to teach it themselves, even if they could get their parishioners interested.

The problem that arises from this lack of education may be put in a succinct image. Harry Emerson Fosdick once suggested that a pastor ought to preach with the Bible in one hand and today's *New York Times* in the other. He makes an important point, and one of which most ministers are aware. Yet there is clearly something missing—namely, the millenia of Christian thought that intervenes between the time the Bible was written and today's newspaper. Where it is missing is in the body of the minister—the head and heart—to which the two hands are attached. This is a problem which the church as a whole has not addressed, since at present the only education that churches actually provide is Sunday School and seminary. It leaves a large gap.

The church is deeply ambivalent about this educational gap. On the one hand, education is a major item in the budgets of most mainline denominations and there are educational requirements for ordination. On the other hand, most of these churches are surprisingly detached from undergraduate education, taking for granted that the church-related colleges can fend for themselves academically and financially. In an effort to be everything to everybody, the money that should be spent on college education is divided among the pressing causes championed by clergy who have had their consciences pricked by needs they feel the church has been remiss in addressing, who cannot live with themselves and the church until they are addressed, such as care for the elderly or soup kitchens. Often these programs are small budget items; in order to finance them, education, a big budget item, is the target of cuts. Tragically, these well-intentioned causes end up whittling away at the very thing the church needs to be sensitive to—its training for mission.

The issue is not just a financial one. The same churches lack any desire to claim the church-related colleges as their own. There is little attempt to become involved in any discussion with the college on how it can best work with the church in its task of educating persons to draw life from the best of intellectual culture and from the transcendent body of Christ, and who bestow life on culture and the church in return. A woeful lack of information persists within many denominations about their own colleges, among clergy and congregations alike. Ministers are as likely as not to send their own children to state universities.

What are the solutions? In order to be lasting and of real value, these solutions must be educational—not simply good will gestures to strengthen the ties of churches with their colleges. They should also take place at two levels, one at the wider denominational level and the other at the parish level, addressing how the clergy may become more effective in transmitting the tradition and how the laity may hear it.

At the highest denominational levels, serious consideration of the church's financial support of the colleges needs to replace what is at present often only token support. Such support can also be more creative than it usually is. For example, endowment of the college chaplaincy or of chairs of philosophy and religion by the denomination, might be considered. Some denominations already do this. Similarly, a denomination could undertake a program to refund that portion of tuition that its students spend on courses in religion, or other courses just as essential to forming an educated and active believer, clergy or lay.

Churches can also be far more imaginative in the educational use they actually make of the schools to which they are tied. Churches, for example, can make better use of their colleges for such things as adult education and continuing education for clergy. Continuing education does *not* mean simply bringing the clergy together on the campuses of the related colleges and then importing a couple of middleweight theologians from the denominational seminary to spar for the benefit of the participants, as is so often done. Instead it means actually using the schools' educational resources, such as the faculty and library of the colleges, to establish programs of continuing education. Not only do the colleges have these resources in religion, they also are well prepared to integrate other fields such as politics, literature and the sciences. All too often ministers spend their allowance for continuing education at a weekend conference, returning home with a reading list and some good intentions. If continuing education could instead be linked to the ongoing program of an educational institution, such as a college, it would provide for the clergy's *evolving* educational development throughout the years of their ministry. Dioceses or presbyteries might even consider putting a minister of continuing education on their staff who, instead of setting up the occasional large conference, could work directly with local clergy, perhaps setting up weekly lunch meetings to discuss books of theological and social interest. Every minister's library is stocked with books that have gone unread for lack of anybody with whom to discuss them.

These programs, or ones like them, demand to be taken seriously by the denominations. An important key to their success in the churches' reclamation of the task of educating their people, however, is the deep involvement of parish ministers. Parish clergy are the most vital element to the church's educational ministry; apart from the seminaries, they tend to *be* that ministry through their efforts to educate the children and adults of their congregations. They are also the ones most affected when the church's educational ministry weakens or fails. They are affected both personally, since their own education will lack depth and focus, and in the quality of their ministry to a congregation that is unaware of the depths of Christian knowledge. Therefore the church's task of reclaiming a ministry of education needs to begin at the parish level.

The church is fortunate in that many well-educated men and women, instead of remaining in academia, have entered the parish ministry. Perhaps the best way of seeing how the task of education begins with individual priests and ministers is to consider what these people give to the church. It is not a model of advanced scholarship to be emulated by everybody—not all clergy should be academics with a call. At their best, they can be examples of focused thought. They do not have to quote Plato and Augustine, that would be pretentious; they can, however, use Plato and Augustine. In this regard, clergy may also be exemplars of a ministry that tries to take the intelligence of the laity seriously. Fosdick exhorted pastors to preach with the *New York Times* in one hand; too many have given their congregations the Sunday comics instead. At first congregations may be tickled by pithy little insights from self-help books and "Peanuts"; in the long run, either they tire of it or they come to understand faith in terms of comics. The church has a responsibility both to give them meat and, also, as St. Paul did, to give them what it takes to eat it. The minister who draws on her own education and continuous reading is giving them just those things.

The laity are not stupid, and ministers need to prepare themselves as deeply as the real needs of a congregation go, if not further. Just as Paderewski, the great Polish pianist, claimed that his public knew when he had not practiced for three days, so too a congregation knows when its pastor has not read a decent book recently—or ever. One pastor observed the importance of this task very well when he told his congregation: " I can't promise to be interesting; I do promise to talk about what is important and that should be interesting enough." He recognized that in order to do this, he had to prepare himself to know what was important.

The first step for the clergy is to address their own education. The task, however, does not stop there. Ministers must also recognize that the church does not educate its young adults very well; it is their task to address that gap, particularly as it affects the lives of their congregation. The various aspects of a college-bound student's decisions about college, his preparation for college, and even his undergraduate life are all part of the job.

Consider, for example, the help a student needs to decide on a college. How do most high school seniors pick a college? What do they expect to get out of education? The answers are barely commensurable with the weight of the choice. College-bound students are usually deluged with information and advice during their senior year in high school. In fact, if they have scored well on college admissions tests and let their names be distributed to colleges seeking highly qualified students, during that year they will probably not go a day without mail from some college that wants *them*. Since they are at an age when they don't receive much mail, they are usually quite impressed with themselves. Despite this massive amount of information, however, most students are woefully under-informed about the goals of higher education. Often they set about choosing the school they eventually will attend on the basis of how it fits with their perceived present wants and individual goals. These will include such things as programs that will lead to the profession they think they want—but probably will not ever actually enter—as well as closeness (or distance) from a boyfriend or girlfriend left behind. Even when they do notice the claims of schools to educate the whole person, they don't know what it means other than possibly they will be well-rounded, capable of nearly anything they choose to do. Such is the wonderful self-centered optimism of youth. Clearly they need their eyes opened, and a minister ought to be able to help.

How can a minister open a student's eyes? The point of much of Christian proclamation and education is to offer an alternative to futile and limited views of personal success. Students, therefore, ought to be asked what they hope to do with their education beyond turning it into a well-paying job. As students choose a form of education that will mold much of their adult lives, they should be prodded into seeing what kind of choice they are making and why. They should also be urged to recognize the various alternatives that exist. Somebody ought to ask them, "What are you choosing for yourself in the long run? Personal gain? A life of wisdom? A life that might help others? What does your future life look like?" Asking these questions is a part of the church's educational ministry. While they may not change anybody's mind about

where to go to school, they might change the spirit in which
a student learns. Parents sometimes ask these questions; high
school counselors rarely do; ministers must.

Asking these questions should be as natural to youth ministry as talking about sex and drugs. That is also to say that
most pastors would find it terribly awkward and embarassing,
a personal matter to be left to conscience. But in a very real
sense these are no different from the questions a minister
should be posing regularly to the congregation as a whole.
They really should flow from a conversation that ought to be
naturally taking place all the time within any congregation.
This is a conversation that began between Jesus and his disciples, which we are simply continuing. How well that conversation goes depends in good part on the minister's own
education, which allows her to ask these questions of herself
and others. When the conversation does not go well, it may
at least underline the need to pose such questions continually from a young age. It may also underline the need for the
minister to draw on her own education; when she does not
have a good one, to do everything in her power to get one.

There is also a great deal of practical help a pastor can give
to college-bound students. Many ministers frequently take
senior high youth groups on visits to the denomination's
schools and make them aware of what the denomination has
to offer. If nothing else, the clergy ought to be aware of these
schools and their programs, although many are not. They
should also be aware of the scholarship possibilities that each
denomination offers to its students and encourage students to
make use of them. In addition they may even offer, as one
minister did, a course to students on how to study, thus
earning him at least some gratitude when his students arrived
at college and found that their high school habits would not
suffice.

The heart of educational ministry, however, does not lie in
practical suggestions. It lies in the constant formation of the
community of faith and the ongoing conversation of that com-

munity. For this reason alone an educational ministry cannot stop once a student has gone off to college, if the idea of community is ever to take any root within a student. Contact with college students is not easy; as they try to gain independence from family, they also tend to put distance between themselves and the church. Just as students need to leave the family to establish their own separate lives, so too do they need to claim faith for themselves. The difference, however, is that the family stays in touch with the student; the church does not always, except perhaps through the family. This neglect tends to reinforce a student's often proud sense of prodigality. Yet the church needs to show continued concern, never to disinherit the prodigal, and this bond can remain alive in a number of ways. One way is to continue the discussion about education begun in high school whenever the student is at home. Another way is to maintain contact through the college itself. One thing that ministers rarely do is to inform the college chaplain (particularly if one knows the chaplain and if the school is denominational) that a parishioner is on campus. Since students on the whole rarely make themselves known to the chaplain, at least the introduction gives him or her the opportunity to make personal contact and show that the church community is not confined to a specific local congregation.

The key is the ongoing conversation; it forms the context of meaning, the sense of community. Little of what one does as a parish minister will show immediate tangible results. This is particularly true in the case of students. The usual age at which students go to college is one where formal religion plays a slighter role in their lives than perhaps at any other time. But it may well be an unusual opportunity for starting a conversation that in the long run may be effective for building up the community. I myself am grateful for the interest and concern of my own pastor, who started in my home congregation while I was in college, for he let me expound all sorts of ideas which were radical to me but undoubtedly stale for him. Nearly twenty years later we still make it a point to meet for lunch whenever we can, a continuing relationship that has become a joy and a benefit for both of us. I have learned a great from the wisdom he has gained from the ministry, and from the poetry he has always loved quoting; he has had the advantage of the years of my own theological study when practical necessities have not always allowed him to follow his own interests as much as he would like. The friendship is one born of mutual concern and respect and is, in a strong sense, the continuation of a conversation begun many years ago. It is, even in its lighter and more irreverent moments, a matter of "two or three gathered in my name."

What is true and helpful for ministers to do, however, should not stop with them. This ministry is also the responsibility of parents, youth group leaders and family friends—if they are really concerned about the transmission of Christian thinking to a new generation. It is, in short, a communal concern because ultimately the community depends upon it.

Chapter Eight

Over the Ivied Walls: The Value of an Education

When I first began teaching I traveled alone to the Midwest, while my wife and daughter followed two weeks later with the furniture. When this plan was first laid I intended to use the long Labor Day weekend to return East and load the Ryder truck and to help move the furniture. When I asked the Dean whether the school actually had Labor Day as a holiday, however, I discovered that the school honored Labor Day by laboring. And thus I labored in the classroom, giving my first lectures, and my wife took a turn at being a cowboy of the road.

Despite the inconvenience for me, the school's decision was perhaps not a bad one. There is a deep connection between labor and education. Education is what prepares us for labor; its effectiveness is gauged by how well it does. Education also can give meaning and purpose to the labor one does for the forty or fifty years after college. In a sense, education is itself a sort of work. Thus the value of an education depends in good part on the labor we do.

In thinking about the relationship between labor and education, it is helpful to recall Augustine's distinction to which I alluded earlier. Everything we do and everything we have can be divided into two groups: the things we have and do for the sake of something else, and the things we enjoy, purely and simply, for their own sake. It is a distinction that can be applied to everything. We use money for what it will buy for us, and we enjoy what we buy. Augustine's distinction also applies to labor, for when we work we do so for the sake of something else—to support our families, to make money, to give us prestige and power.

The distinction is fairly clear and obvious. What is not clear, however, is exactly what things *ought* to be used and what things *ought* to be enjoyed. Too often, as we all know, we use our money for things that do not give us lasting happiness and too often what we labor for does not bestow joy. At times, we take something such as money, which is meant only to be used, and end up trying to enjoy it for its own sake. There is no more pitiful picture of degraded humanity than the miser who will not buy a new shirt because he will not part with his money. Howard Hughes, we are told, spent the last years of his life in a single room in filthy squalor despite his millions. Yet what is equally distressing is when we possess something worth enjoying, but put it to some purpose that is not.

Now clearly there are both people who hate their work and people who find a great deal of meaning in it. Of those who are dissatisfied, many have every reason; there are jobs in which the conditions are horrendous, the pay abysmal, and the respect nonexistent. But there are many who are dissatisfied because they have no idea of what place their job has in the scheme of things. They are not dissatisfied because the job itself is bad, but because what they "use" the job for seems pointless and unenjoyable. So their dissatisfaction with a job is only part of a general lack of enjoyment of life itself. Such people simply do not see what use their labor has, or else they can see no purpose in the uses to which they have put it. Simone Weil observed during a year working in three Paris factories that chief among the factors contributing to affliction is the sense that our labor serves no purpose we can see. When she went on to make suggestions about how labor might be reformed to be more humane, Weil put at the top of her list that the purpose of a worker's efforts always be transparent

to him. Her insights have been confirmed by numerous remarks made by the American workers whom Studs Terkel in-
terviewed for *Working*. They are also confirmed by the many
people who work hard, are not paid much, but really enjoy
what they do. They enjoy it because it serves a larger purpose.
Labor is to be used for something else, and that goal is what
makes it meaningful. The enjoyment of the goal comes to permeate the labor, as it were, and makes it enjoyable.

Something similar can be said about education. Education
is valuable chiefly as a means to something else; and our
ability to enjoy it depends upon our ability to press education
into the service of something higher. Just as the worth of any
sort of labor is justified by its capacity to be used for something more ultimate, so too should education be justified by
that for which it is used. Ideally the goal in both cases coin-
cides, since education does fit us for our labor. A musician,
for example, should get out of her education an ability to play;
from her playing she should get enjoyment—an enjoyment
for which her education has also fitted her.

This similarity between education and labor is not difficult
to recognize. Less easy to see are all the ways in which education plays the role of a stepping stone to meaningful labor.
What is generally assumed, particularly among the students
most anxious to find jobs, is that the relationship is strictly a
pragmatic one. And this is partly true. For education does
train us to do a particular job and enables us to play a specific
role. Our education may even turn out to be a proving ground
for our chosen vocation, a chance to test our future plans. If
I hate mathematics and struggle painfully and futilely with
the subject in college, I am going to recognize that a career
in computer science is not in the cards. The movie "Superman
III" opens with Richard Pryor, unemployed, taking a computer science course in the grand hope of making big bucks.
The next scene, in a wonderful piece of irony, shows him
punching keys on a computer in a long room that has rows of
terminals with dozens of other people doing exactly the same

thing. In this movie, he goes on to be a brilliant computer crook; what is worth contemplating, however, is that room. If you do not like such rooms, but show little aptitude for doing much more in a given field, you would wisely stop after a few courses and rethink your career goals. More positively, education can also open our eyes to careers we have been blind to before, simply through the enjoyment of learning their preliminary steps in the classroom.

This practical relationship between education and labor, however, is not the only one, though few may recognize that fact. Education is also vital in empowering us to see what sort of labor is valuable and to give us some sense of what is really ultimate. Far from merely training us for labor, it also makes us see what real use labor has. It is for this reason that education needs such things as philosophy and theology, even if they do not seem "practical." By causing us to examine our deepest assumptions about the world, they force us to perceive more clearly what is truly valuable.

An excellent illustration of this point comes from the ancient Greeks. Aristotle tells the story of the first Greek philosopher, Thales, who became so preoccupied with a study of the heavens that he absentmindedly fell into a well. A maidservant, standing by, said that Thales was so eager to know what was happening in the sky that he could not see what lay at his feet. Aristotle, however, points out that Thales was not completely inept. For later, upon observing from the stars that the season's weather was going to be especially propitious, he went and hired all the oil presses in the region far before harvest time. When a bumper crop came in, he became a very rich man because he held the monopoly of all the region's oil presses. Now one point of this story may be that philosophical knowledge can be turned to material advantage. Yet there is another point as well. Remember that Thales did not go on to become an oil merchant, but continued to study the stars.

What philosophy did for Thales was to show him what was really worth his effort. Thus the real value of education may lie less in its ability to fit us for jobs and more in its power to let us see what is valuable. It is not likely that most liberal arts students who are obliged to take poetry will become poets, but poetry is still important; it makes sense out of both the work we actually do and the life we lead when we are not working.

Education is not merely what we use to reach our goals; more importantly, it shapes—and sometimes creates—our goals. It is not a stepping stone we leave behind, but a tool we carry with us for a lifetime of sorting and evaluating our past and our future. And in the course of its use, it is even reflected back on itself so that we begin to see it in a new and different light. Just as teachers give us not only tools to operate in the world but standards by which to evaluate teaching, so too education in general gives us the means to assess what we have learned and what we ought to learn in the future. It also gives us the means, good or poor, for future learning. What we learn from becoming a part of a tradition and culture is more than facts and theories; it is a way of thought that seeks to rejuvenate itself in the present.

Important as it is to recognize this side of education, it is still a mere ideal. Neither culture nor education is that simple. Students do not enter college a blank slate, but with a mind previously shaped by habits of thought and with plenty of values already firmly entrenched. The generation of college students who are so keen on using education to prepare themselves for careers do not think of education carelessly or randomly, but have very definite purposes for their education in service of these intended careers. This makes the task of higher education far more complicated. A student's experience of the culture as well as her previous educational experiences will all go to evaluate and shape what she learns in college. As one student asked his teacher in a critical thinking course, "Are you going to mess with my head?" He meant, I suppose, that he had little intention of changing his mind.

Students thus pick and choose their higher education courses pretty much in accord with their present purposes; changes in the shape of education need to be seen in that context.

A second complication arises when we remember that schools themselves are not exempt from cultural trends. They do not enshrine the wisdom of a tradition in the same way that the tables of the law were preserved whole in the ark of the covenant, with protective powers that threatened any who would desecrate them. Rather, colleges and universities are a part of an ongoing culture that often pulls many ways at once. Cultures operate simultaneously on at least two different levels—one is the broad continuing tradition, the other is the temporary popular level, which may or may not have anything to contribute to cultural wisdom. This gives schools a dual task. On the one hand they must reflect upon how to shape viable and worthwhile purposes for students. On the other hand, they also need to examine their own deep-seated assumptions about what is useful and what is enjoyable about education. For often they may have covered mere pragmatic assumptions with ancient ivy, not recognizing that there are these two levels of culture.

In *Habits of the Heart* Robert Bellah provides a fascinating study of American individualism that is helpful in discovering how middle-class Americans talk about and justify their life decisions, that is, how they view ultimate purposes. His observations are helpful for understanding the uses to which we put higher education, particularly when we examine the rhetoric used to justify education. Americans tend to express what they think is valuable in terms of "personal self-fulfillment," Bellah and his colleagues argue; they are "determined to press ahead with the task of letting go of all other criteria other than radical private validation."[15] It does not mean they are completely selfish, for many Americans do find a great deal of fulfillment in family and community involvement. An important part of the American character, this individualism lies at the base of our form of democracy, where it is expected that the individual pursuit of happiness will cause us to form political alliances and compromises for the common good.

How does this affect the way that we view education? Education is valuable to the extent that it can contribute to self-fulfillment, whether it is through training in the skills necessary to find rewarding labor or by giving adults those things needed to enjoy the fruits of their labor in leisure time. There is a certain wonderful pragmatic efficiency to this attitude, for the value of an education is easily proved and colleges, insofar as they share this view, quickly respond to the social needs that education ought to fulfill.

This is more than mere surmise. Colleges *do* tend to view education this way, as an examination of their appeals to prospective students proves. A great deal of effort goes into publicizing how effectively a college can fill these needs of the self. For example, one recruitment tactic employed by numerous colleges features quotes by recent successful graduates stating how valuable their education has been. Traditional liberal arts courses, such as those in the fine arts, are advertised with a stress on the development of individual creative talents. Illinois College, for example, heads the narrative section of a brochure for prospective fine arts students with the title: "Nurturing Individual Talents." Hardly daring, this may perhaps even be a slightly conservative approach. Philosophy courses are marketed by departmental members eager for students as excellent pre-law training. In fact, the American Philosophical Association itself promotes philosophy as a major by showing statistics which prove the superior scores of philosophy majors on standardized graduate school admissions tests, such as the Graduate Record Examination and Law School Admissions Test. Departments of "Communications" and "Business Administration" are now regular departments in many liberal arts colleges and feature prominently in the school's promotional material. Such advertising is not a baited hook; it is revealing of how prospective students and colleges justify educational choices, often unconsciously. It is one more proof of the fact that we as a people do justify things in this way. If self-fulfillment is *the* language we use to justify decisions and positions, as Bellah suggests it is, there is no real alternative.

Most colleges would argue that they do not encourage selfishness. At the same time they are nurturing individual talents, they also provide a much needed, more expansive, sense of self and fulfillment for their graduates. Some years ago William Norris, the chairman of Control Data, suggested in an article in *The Chronicle of Higher Education* that business needs liberal arts graduates. Corporate executives are fed up with unimaginative business majors; they want people with more creativity who can see the larger issues. Liberal arts colleges have not hesitated to trumpet this, claiming that they give this creativity— thus proving their value in truly improving the lives of graduates. They also regularly point to studies which indicated that while business majors tend to get jobs faster than traditional liberal arts majors, within five years the latter are holding the better jobs. They are simply better able to make creative use of possibilities.

Is this increased creativity enough to let us see what is to be enjoyed? Is it sufficient to combat the alienating structures that individualism has, ironically, brought with it? Bellah's diagnosis suggests that it is not, for our alienation is less a problem of a self's limited creativity and more a problem of getting beyond ourselves. Because there does not seem to be a common language for justifying our work and actions beyond that of individual self-fulfillment, we find that we are unable to form meaningful communities; instead, we now have, as Bellah calls it, "life style enclaves." Even when there are attempts to form communities, people struggle to say what these communities are and why they are important, or they delude themselves about what exactly the community is. The sense of a larger whole and a common good to which all are expected to contribute is largely disappearing.

American churches fare no better. Even they have a difficult time convincing parishioners that the body of Christ is bigger than they are and participation in the life of the church is not simply a personal option. Many, in fact, have given up trying to convince anybody of this and have simply embraced personal fulfillment. In a recent conversation another Presbyterian minister told me that faith is meant to bring us health and wealth. When I suggested that this would mean that Jesus' preaching of the kingdom was a metaphor for the fulfillment of the middle-class American dream, he disagreed. He thought it meant the fulfillment of the *upper-class* dream.

Christianity, of course, is naturally concerned about this tendency to justify thought and action strictly by reference to personal fulfillment, since Christianity at its best has always understood the ends of human beings in the light of a community. Yet the present mood of our society makes it difficult for that message to be heard. But the church's concern is not limited by this problem alone; there is a deep religious problem as well, as the exaltation of the individual comes very close to being a rival religion. As the conversation above shows, it has little to do with what Jesus taught. Those fundamentalists who accuse the secular humanists of embracing a rival religion know this; they recognize the tendency in American education and culture to make human values self-sufficient, without reference to anything higher. In this sense, individualism has Pelagian overtones: it assumes that the highest of human goals are attainable by our own unaided efforts—if we believe hard enough in ourselves. At its most optimistic, it also fails to come to grips with the real ability of human beings to fail.

One place where communities *are* being developed, Bellah suggests, is among the fundamentalists. Yet even they have not entirely succeeded. For their communities tend to be ingrown, rarely looking to any sort of larger community with other Christians—including the historical "communion of saints." According to Bellah, these communities have "no larger memory of how Christians have coped with the world historically,"[16] which leaves them without adequate resources to deal with the larger culture. Thus even they find it difficult to get beyond their own narrow confines.

Creativity, an expanded sense of self, fulfillment—none of these is sufficient. They may even exacerbate the problem. They can create additional problems within education itself, as students and faculty by cultivating them unwittingly come to accept individualism as the only means of finding what is enjoyable. A correlation of the researches carried out by Bellah's team with Allan Bloom's cranky observations about the reign of relativism in American colleges suggests this has happened. In a society where opinions and decisions are justified purely by reference to the self, and where there is no overarching sense of a community to which one is responsible, relativism can hardly be avoided. Bloom has complained that we are witnessing a loss of reason in higher education, that students are committed relativists who refuse to acknowledge any authority higher than personal opinion. Small wonder. Reason is a communal and historical matter, the one truly common possession of a community. When there is no sense of community it stands to reason that reason will not be the means of persuasion. It is in this regard that Bloom's idea that education *should* be an alternative to the idols of popular culture must be taken seriously. Education does not have to criticize the shallowness of culture, which is often an act often of intellectual arrogance, but to provide an alternative to uprooting and alienating tendencies within the culture itself—and within education.

On a superficial level, the needed alternative is fairly obvious—a greater appreciation of the importance of communities. But how are we going to grasp that alternative? There are three crucial elements. The first is simply presenting an alternative suited to the problem. Second, the solution cannot be abstract; it has to be concrete and accessible to us. In this regard I want to suggest that for any solution to be effective it has to draw upon some part of a "story" that is familiar to us, even if the story has been neglected. For example, while American society may be excessively individualistic, it nevertheless does have a republican and biblical tradition that emphasizes community. We have roots in that tradition on which we can draw. Similarly American churches may also emphasize the individual, but clearly they have roots in a Christianity which from the time of Paul has emphasized the importance of the body. They need to draw on these roots to reorient themselves, to regain a deeper sense of their identity and mission. Third, we need education to recover those roots. We need it both in order to know what they are and to help us to draw life from them.

For a moment I would like to look at Augustine's *City of God* to see where the ultimate value of an education lies. It is a good example of how these three elements are related, for it shows not only an alternative rooted in a common story but how education discovers it. Augustine wrote the *City of God* when the "eternal" city of Rome was first sacked by the barbarians. At that time the Roman citizens began to murmur among themselves that the cause of this unspeakable disaster was the official Christian status of the Roman state. Because of their new religion the Romans had neglected the worship of their traditional, indigenous gods; the gods who had made Rome great and protected it in the past.

It was in response to these charges that Augustine wrote his very long work, seeking to show that they were groundless. He pointed out to the Romans that in the past they had not always paid very careful attention to their own gods; for that matter, even when they had, the gods had not always protected Rome. Although it took Augustine literally hundreds of pages to make this point, it was well taken. Yet a reader might still observe that after all these pages Augustine had still not shown why Christianity in its turn had not protected Rome from her attackers. Why was Christianity the best alternative, especially since the outcome was the same?

What makes the *City of God* a great book instead of an overly long piece of late Roman rhetoric is Augustine's response to this question. Rather than trying to show how Christianity could protect Rome, Augustine claimed that there are actually two cities—the city of this world, represented by Rome, and the city of God. Each city is composed of people bound together by a common love. If one wants to see what the character of each city is, one only has to look at what they love most and at the fruits that love has borne. Augustine argues that the city of God is inhabited by those who love God and seek to follow him, while the earthly city is made up of those who love the things and ways of the world and who find their security there. Thus there was never any question of Christianity seeking to make Roman power eternal. If God did not protect Roman power, it was because Roman power was not the be-all and end-all of God's purposes. The workings of God's eternal plan were not going to grind to a halt merely in order to to rescue Rome from the traps of its own devising.

The importance of Augustine's *City of God* has always been well recognized, but it was a scholar of this century, C.N. Cochrane, who put his finger on what Augustine had done. He had provided society with an alternative to the means it had traditionally used to solve its problems. Whereas Virgil in the *Aeneid* had given Rome a story by which they could understand that their destiny was to conquer and control the world, Augustine had delved into the biblical story to give the defeated Romans and their descendants a new way by which they could understand themselves. It was not a way of power and domination.

For us Augustine provides an excellent example of what a true alternative may be. Rather than simply accepting the question in the form that the Romans wanted to ask it, and thus accepting their answer as well, he moved both question and answer to a higher plane, a move that was both unexpected and revelatory. But there is more to the *City of God* than this. The fact is that Augustine did not actually propose a completely new alternative to Rome, or one totally outside Roman culture. Instead he drew on a story that was already familiar to many in the Roman Empire, which had embraced Christianity for over one hundred years. Although Christianity was relatively new in the Empire, it was not unheard of; already it was a significant part of the culture. To many people it must not have been very clear exactly how Christianity fit into established Roman patterns; it was Augustine's genius to use the biblical story to reunify a culture that had lost its center.

Augustine's achievement in the *City of God* (as well as the questions he raises) cannot be fully appreciated, however, until we realize something further. What allowed him to raise these questions, and why did they continue to be crucial questions for the society that came after him? It was his own education and his writings on education, especially the work *On Christian Teaching*, where he makes the distinction between things to be used and things to be enjoyed. Augustine had himself been educated within the late Roman liberal arts tradition, which aimed at philosophy, or, more accurately, wisdom. Upon his conversion Augustine under took to write a series of works on the liberal arts, and towards towards the end of his life he returned to finish it. The years of episcopal care and preaching—and biblical study—showed through in the finished product; while he still assumed the context of the Roman liberal arts and its *paideia*, he had given it a new heart, namely, the Bible. Rather than using the liberal arts as a direct means of coming to know God, he now explained the value of these arts as helping people to read the Bible, which, in turn, is valuable for knowing God. The change must be viewed as a reflection of his own changing experience in attempting to know "God and the soul," but we must also see it in another light. The new vision of *paideia* that Augustine himself had undertaken was what allowed him to come to the insights he did. The striking alternative Augustine presented to traditional Roman society was achieved not by a sudden flash of unexpected creative insight, but by his deliberate absorption of the biblical story—which Augustine placed at the heart of education and used to absorb the liberal arts tradition. His entire educational system was based on that story and it allowed him to see questions about Roman culture in a different light.

Education functions in Augustine in a number of important ways, all of which signal its importance. In the first place, as he tells us in the *Confessions*, it was his education that set him on a quest for wisdom, a quest he never doubted. After his conversion that education began anew with a different center—the Bible. And through that biblically centered education he was able to discover the alternative that Roman society so desperately need. Finally, it was his Christian liberal arts, reformed from the Roman version, which served as the means by which he was able to apply his social agenda effectively. In all these cases we can see that education is at its most valuable when it allows us to see possibilities for leading our lives that we would not have seen otherwise. In our own situation, we might hope to find an education capable of putting the idea of personal fulfillment in some context of ultimacy, one that would lead us to question the limited goals we may have unconsciously accepted.

In order that education might effect this revaluation for us, however, it needs to see itself somewhat differently than it presently does. I strongly suspect that most people—including educators—see education as a matter of "enlightenment," which like the age of the Enlightenment posits as its ideal the knowledgeable, autonomous person who becomes more autonomous the more he knows. If this is the picture under which we are operating, then the task of combatting excessive individualism would be one of raising consciousness about our need for communities. Yet in the final analysis this is no different than the creative businessman who has an expanded sense of self; it leaves our fundamental view of the individual intact without challenging it. Noting that political and economic liberalism rests on a story of human beings as essentially selfish, that liberalism merely tries to put this selfishness to everybody's advantage, Stanley Hauerwas claims that with this story about human beings it ought to be no surprise that in the end liberalism produces selfish people. Similarly an Enlightenment view of knowledge that promotes the ideal of the autonomous knowledgeable person will produce people who try for autonomy—even if they talk knowledgeably about the need for communities. As personnel managers, these people see no problem in trying to develop an *esprit de corps* among workers to enhance productivity while at the same time trying to climb the corporate ladder themselves.

The alternative story for education is one which recognizes the larger context—the body—in which human lives are lived. It is a vision of education that does not promote community with mere words, but emphasizes the truly communal nature of education. It recognizes that communities are not only a desirable end-product of education but the very context of education—whether through learning together socially and intellectually, or through conversations with thinkers and problems of the past, present and future. This is not an unheard of story for us; it is at the root of both our biblical heritage and our Greek heritage of *paideia*.

How can we have an education like this?

One way we can have it is by recognizing something more about the relationship of education to work, namely, that education is itself work and can be related directly to some higher purpose just as any other form of labor. That relationship is one that comes from making education both the work of discovering purpose and the work of reorienting one's life to fit it. Education, in this sense, is not simply practice for life, but the living of life; not only the shaper of goals, but the living of them as well.

Many college graduates will speak wistfully of a wasted college education and wish aloud that it could be repeated. At times this undoubtedly means that they wish they had applied themselves in order to acquire skills they now wish they had. Yet perhaps even more often what is meant is that they wish they had lived better as students, so that they could continue in adult life to shape and reshape their lives. What they are beginning to see is that education is not a mere task that is finished at graduation, but a lifelong labor of seeking what is best and shaping one's life around it. Bound to limited aspirations, they no longer seem able to do that; they do not even know now how to aspire.

If education itself is to be meaningful work, part of its task involves relating the student to a larger context to which she can orient herself, a context at once communal and individual. But "relating" is perhaps a poor choice of terms if it is taken to mean that education performs some kind of external operation on her. Perhaps a better way of putting it is to say that education furnishes a place for her to be part of a larger context where her actions make sense, both as a person and as part of a community. Academic bodies must be social communities of common purpose, to which each member may contribute and find fulfillment in doing so. But the same body also must be a community of conversation—not only with itself but also with a larger tradition that gives it its links to the world.

Few baccalaureate sermons or commencement speeches are particularly memorable. I do remember one line, however, during my own graduation that has stuck in my memory and illustrates very well the degree to which education and its community are a work of joy. The speaker simply remarked, "Most people will tell you that upon your graduation you are about to enter the real world. It would be well for you to remember that Plato thought it was the most unreal world of all."

It was, of course, a true remark; what passes for reality in the larger world is often little more than a shadow-judging contest. But the remark went beyond the merely critical. It did not imply that we alone beheld the sun, especially since we were not given that day the trite charge to change the world before the next class had graduated and we became the problem. Instead its truth drew upon our own educational experience to see that what we had done in four years was not irrelevant to what we would do in the future.

Four years earlier we had each entered the college with our own prejudices, confusions and limited visions. We each had what amounted to our own language; we could barely talk to each other. But by the end of four years something had happened. We had learned to talk to each other, our cliques which had been personal refuges had broken up and we became a class. We had also learned to talk to our teachers, including those who had written the great books we had read. In some sense, therefore, we had built a community and cared for a common good. We had, in short, learned something about what is real, and it was not what we entered with. None of us would have gone back to what we had been. The value of our education had become apparent to us even as we were being educated and before we applied for jobs. In this the work of education had become a joy and had justified itself, even without reference to our vocations.

It is not a matter of naivete or nostalgia to suggest that years later we were trying to recreate that world. There is, of course, always nostalgia for one's college years. But even that nostalgia, when it is not entirely backward-looking, witnesses to the value of education. For the sense of community and shared thought that is gained through education is something that affects our ideals. One does not simply try to create that community all over again, but rather uses it as a model for constructing new communities. One gains a sense that community is important; then it is important to find and enter a community where our work makes sense and we enter into conversation with others. In this regard the conversations of college become the model for further conversations, and the books shared are used to break down the walls that forbid conversation. Because we had learned to converse with a tradition that was bigger than our personal visions, we learned to talk in general. And thus we were able in time to discover some very non-traditional and non-Western ideas. We had only read great books of the West, few of which were contemporary. Yet they became the beginning of a conversation which led us in later life to talk seriously with the non-Western world and with the contemporary world. I can honestly say that if I never had to read the Sermon on the Mount in Greek I probably never would have read the Bhagavad-Gita.

When at the end of her life Simone Weil began meditating on the problem of rootedness, undoubtedly she did so because she felt that the culture of her native France had become uprooted. She believed that contemporary France had lost important traditional values, especially communal values, a loss that fragmented and weakened her as all authority came to be centered in an impersonal bureaucratic state. The growing of roots, Weil thought, could correct that. Yet if this is all that she was thinking about, it was a conservative, even reactionary, project. Weil, however, had a much larger vision. The growing of roots not only leads to greater cultural coherence, and thus greater coherence for individual lives, it also allows us to approach the cultures of other people with respect and seriousness. The relativism of purely personal fulfillment goes hand in hand with a narrow nationalism; neither can appreciate anything beyond what touches the self. If, however, we can appreciate the real values of our own communities we have a way by which to appreciate the values of others.

The sort of education we need might very well take a cue from Weil's notion of rootedness. We need an education that will aid us in inheriting our tradition, especially those elements that can awaken us from solipsistic dreams of autonomy. We need to go through the very act of inheriting, so that we really do become part of something larger. From that act our perspective cannot help but be truly enlarged.

Throughout this book I have not spoken about many of our most pressing contemporary problems, such as racism, sexism, the need to learn about other cultures and religions, the nuclear threat, all of which are high on the contemporary educational agenda. If I have not dealt with them it is not because they are not important—they are. Yet in order to address them we need something more than mere knowledge about oppressed peoples and the facts about nuclear war to frighten us into action. We need a sense of value that can only come from belonging together. How else, for example, could a white man understand what a black man is saying? If belonging is not a conscious value for the white man, but self-fulfillment is, and there are no *legal* barriers to black achievement, he can't understand when the black man talks about being excluded. If the white man does have a sense of the value of being a part of the whole, there might be a chance he could hear. But he will not have that sense merely by being told about it, he has to live it. We need an education that will help us to live it.

The growing of roots is crucial for gaining any sense of belonging to a larger whole. Yet, as Weil observed, not all that we might inherit from the past is equally helpful. She herself thought that we have relied too much on vicious Roman imperial practices as a social and cultural model. Those practices, Weil believed, had uprooted the far better early Christian models such as Paul gives in his metaphor of the church as Christ's body. Paul's image does not hide personal autonomy under the cloak of communal righteousness; it genuinely seeks a relation of people to each other and seeks to root the community in the one who is ultimate. These are the models we must regain. Whether or not our present culture can do so is open to speculation. Nevertheless the community that calls itself Christ's body has an imperative to recapture them, for the sake of its own identity and as part of its lasting gift to the cultures in which it finds itself.

Notes

1. Quoted in *The State Journal Register*, Springfield, Illinois, March 15, 1987.

2. Statistics are taken for the most part from William C. Ringenberg, *The Christian College: A History of Protestant Higher Education in America*, Grand Rapids, 1984, Eerdmans

3. For an excellent discussion of the *sensus communis* see Hans-Georg Gadamer, *Truth and Method*, New York, 1986, Crossroad pp.19-29.

4. Jacques Maritain, *Education at the Crossroads*, New Haven, 1943, Yale University Press, p. 1.

5. T.S. Eliot, *Christianity and Culture*, New York, 1968, Harcourt, Brace, Jovanovich, p.105

6. T.S. Eliot, "Modern Education and the Classics," in *Selected Essays*, New York, 1932, Harcourt, Brace and World, p.460

7. Gadamer, *Truth and Method*, p.143

8. Christopher Lasch, *The Culture of Narcissism*, New York, 1979, Warner Books, p.287

9. Northrop Frye, "The Expanding World of Metaphor," in *Journal of the American Academy of Religion*, Dec., 1985 p.594

10. Immanuel Kant, *The Critique of Pure Reason*, B 805-6

11. The *trivium* was composed of the arts of grammar, logic and rhetoric; the *quadrivium* of the arts of music, astronomy, harmony and arithmetic.

12. Blaise Pascal, *Pensees*, 233 (Modern Library Edition, New York, 1941, Random House, p.83)

13. Christopher Derrick, *Escape From Scepticism*, Peru, IL, 1977, Sherwood Sugden, p.26.

14. George Bernanos, *Diary of a Country Priest*, translated Pamela Morris, New York, 1937, Macmillan

15. Robert Bellah, *Habits of the Heart*, New York, 1986, Harper and Row, p.79

16. Bellah, *Habits of the Heart*, p.232

Bibliography

Aristotle, *Nichomachean Ethics*; *Politics* VII.13-VIII.7

Augustine, *The Teacher, On Christian Teaching, On Divine Providence*

Barzun, J., *Teacher in America*, Boston, 1945, Brown, Littlefield

Bellah, R., *Habits of the Heart*, New York, 1985, Harper & Row

Blanshard, B., *The Uses of a Liberal Education*, LaSalle,IL, 1973, Open Court

Bloom, A., *The Closing of the American Mind*, New York, 1987, Simon and Schuster

Bonaventure, *De Reductione Artium ad Theologiam*, trans. Sr. E.T. Healey, Vol. 1 of *The Works of Bonaventure*, St. Bonaventure, NY, 1955, The Franciscan Institute

Cochrane, C.N., *Christianity and Classical Culture*, London, 1944, Oxford University Press

Culler, D., *The Imperial Intellect: A Study of Newman's Educational Ideal*, New Haven, 1955, Yale University Press

Darkey, W.,ed., *Three Dialogues on Liberal Education*, Annapolis, 1979, St. John's College Press

Derrick, C., *Escape From Scepticism: Liberal Education as if Truth Mattered*, Peru, IL, 1977, Sherwood Sugden

Dewey, J., *On Education: Selected Writings*, Chicago, 1964, University of Chicago Press

———*A Common Faith*, New Haven, 1934, Yale University Press

Dykstra, C., *Vision and Character: A Christian Educator's Alternative to Kohlberg*, New York, 1981, Paulist Press

Eliot, T.S., *Christianity and Culture*, New York, 1968, Harcourt, Brace, Jovanovich

———"Modern Education and the Classics," in *Selected Essays*, New York, 1940, Harcourt, Brace and World

Evans, G.R., *Old Arts and New Theology*, Oxford, 1980, Oxford University Press

Farley, E., *Theologia: The Fragmentation and Unity of Theological Education*, Philadelphia, 1983, Fortress Press

Fuller, E., ed. *The Christian Idea of Education*, New Haven, 1957, Yale University Press

Gadamer, H-G., *Truth and Method*, New York, 1986, Crossroad

Groome, T., *Christian Religious Education*, New York, 1980, Harper & Row

Hauerwas, S., *A Community of Character*, Notre Dame, 1981, University of Notre Dame Press

Hirsch, E.D., *Cultural Literacy*, New York, 1987, Houghton Mifflin Co.

Hugh of St. Victor, *The Didascalion of Hugh of St. Victor*, trans. J. Taylor, New York, 1961, Columbia University Press

Jaeger, W., *Paideia: The Ideals of Greek Culture*, 3 vols., trans. G. Highet, New York, 1939 (1945), 1943, 1944, Oxford University Press

———*Early Christianity and Greek Paideia*, New York, 1961, Oxford University Press

Jordan, M., *Ordering Wisdom: The Hierarchy of Philosophical Discourses in Aquinas*, Notre Dame, 1986, University of Notre Dame Press

Lasch, C., *The Culture of Narcissism*, New York, 1979, Warner Books

Lewis, C.S., *The Abolition of Man*, New York, 1947, Macmillan

Maritain, J., *Education at the Crossroads*, New Haven, 1943, Yale University Press

Marrou, H-I., *S. Augustin et la fin de la culture antique*, Paris, 1938, E. Boccard

———*A History of Education in Antiquity*, trans. G. Lamb, Madison, 1982, University of Wisconsin Press

Montaigne, "Of the Education of Children," in *Montaigne: Selected Essays*, New York, 1949, Random House

Newman, J.H., *The Idea of a University*, Notre Dame, 1980, University of Notre Dame Press

Niebuhr, H.R., *Christ and Culture*, New York, 1951, Harper & Row

Pascal, B., *Pensees*, trans. W.F. Trotter, New York, 1941, Random House

Plato, *Meno, Phaedrus, Republic, Laws*

Putnam, H., *Reason, Truth and History*, Cambridge, 1981, Cambridge University Press

Ringenberg, W., *The Christian College: A History of* Protestant Higher Education in America, Grand Rapids, 1984, Eerdmans

Rousseau, J-J., *Emile*, trans. A. Bloom, New York, 1979, Basic Books

Schleiermacher, *Brief Outline on the Study of Theology*, trans. T. Tice, Atlanta, 1977, John Knox Press

Weil. S., *The Need for Roots*, trans. A. Wills, New York, 1952, Harper & Row

Whitehead, A.N., *The Aims of Education and Other Essays*, New York, 1927, Macmillan

Wittgenstein, L., *Culture and Value*, trans. P. Winch, Chicago, 1980, University of Chicago Press